BASKETBALL HISTORY in *Syracuse*

BASKETBALL HISTORY in Syracuse

HOOPS ROOTS

Mark Allen Baker

Charleston · London

THE
History
PRESS

Published by The History Press
Charleston, SC 29403
www.historypress.net

First published 2010

Manufactured in the United States

ISBN 978.1.59629.983.2

Baker, Mark Allen.
Basketball history in Syracuse : hoops roots / Mark Allen Baker.
p. cm.
Includes bibliographical references and index.
ISBN 978-1-59629-983-2
1. Basketball--New York (State)--Syracuse--History. 2. School sports--New York (State)--
Syracuse--History. I. Title.
GV885.73.S97B35 2010
796.32309747'66--dc22
2010033158

Notice: The information in this book is true and complete to the best of our knowledge. It is offered without guarantee on the part of the author or The History Press. The author and The History Press disclaim all liability in connection with the use of this book.

To every son fortunate enough to have a father, like I do, who loves the game of basketball—a diversion to some, a lifestyle in Syracuse!

CONTENTS

PREFACE

A great poet, with whom I had the pleasure of corresponding often, once affirmed to me that both historical and poetic sense should not be contradictory, for if the latter is the little myth we make then the former is the monumental mythos we live—and, in doing so, constantly remake. To that I penned to Red (Robert Penn) Warren: "But history must be written of, by and for the survivors, perhaps as an obligatory part of the grieving process, but more likely as an archive for posterity."

You see, before the Armory Square district was settled, and prior to the construction of the State Fair Coliseum, even in advance of the pouring of the concrete roof for the Onondaga War Memorial and the feasibility analysis for the Carrier Dome, the game of "basket ball" existed in Central New York. That fact still surprises some people—prompting this hardwood allegorist to debunk the disbelief.

It was played by athletes, no less gifted or dedicated than those today. These basketball players—or "basket ball" pioneers, if you wish—executed the game with precision and, in some cases, took the game to extraordinary new levels of performance.

Not long after the Civil War (1861–65), less than thirty years in fact, the game was being taught right here in Central New York, during gym class at Cornell University–Ithaca, located a mere sixty miles south of Syracuse. It was as captivating as it was corporal. The dissemination of the game, augmented by its popularity, even yielded a professional league being played in the neighboring state of New Jersey (1898).

A dapper John A.R. Scott, the first official coach of a program at Syracuse University (1903), quickly noted the game's relevance and embraced it. It was a historic event, dedicated to a sport that contributed to our physical fitness and our well-being. Watching him command his team up and down the court inside the Archbold Gym at the campus "on the hill" was fascinating to observers. By the time Scott's term concluded in 1911, viewers of the game had more options.

Fans gathered at the games of the New York State League, in hamlets like Schenectady, Cohoes and Utica, or across the state at frequent barnstorming events. Gymnasiums and armories were quick to spotlight caged contests that could draw devotees during the seemingly endless and cold winter months. It was during the frosty February of that same year (1911) that 2,800 fans at the Mohawk Armory (less than seventy miles from downtown Syracuse) witnessed the 31st Separate Company team defeat the Buffalo Germans—an event that put an end to a 111-game winning streak and may have been one of the best basketball games ever played.

Prompted by a Syracuse sports editor, some local stars tackled inside the Armory for a few bucks beginning in 1919. "Hill Cagers," names such as Schwarzer, Crisp, Rafter and Casey, did their share to promote the sport they enjoyed, but it remained an avocation.

By the Roaring Twenties, and in a testament to their popularity, we had already been drinking a brand of spring tonic water endorsed by the New York Wanderers (originally the Twenty-third Street YMCA club, a basketball team) for nearly two decades. While the netting, or metal caging, could sustain a fan, it could not intimidate commercialism, the latter being an acknowledged divertissement. Familiar faces, such as local boy Vic Hanson from Central High School and St. John's Manlius, captured headlines, as did the teams they played for. Later, Syracuse standout Wilmeth Sidat-Singh even barnstormed into our own neighborhood. We marveled at their athletic prowess, their seamless integration of mind and sport. To think that this activity, just an enjoyable form of amusement, could actually become an occupation—at least for some—was beyond our imagination.

Basketball leagues emerged from everywhere, or so it seemed, as common as a winter wind blowing around the Jefferson Street Armory. In fact, it was inside that very facility, which transformed itself into an arms cache of a different sort, that we witnessed the All-Americans against visitors, and Reds, not reddish-yellow, soon follow suit. But this was prior to our Nationals—"Danny's Boys," as they were affectionately known. When the Nats took to the court, as part of what would become the sport's premier league, it was basketball at its finest: genuine "Hardwood Heroes and Legends," and they were here, right here, in Syracuse. They even won a championship and our hearts. But before most of us realized just how special they were, they were gone.

Now Philadelphia may well have been Sheboygan back in the fall of 1963, as we shifted our basketball interests to where we had found solace before, "on the hill." There "pre-cagers," some distracted by academics, were sowing the seeds of hardwood dreams—a rim reverie to most, a reality to few. From Addison, Anthony and Bing to Warrick, Washington and Watkins, their predecessors had cleared a path—a course forged by Biasone, Borgmann and Cervi; shaped by Greer, Hannum and Lloyd; and polished by Schayes, Yardley and Boeheim. If the meeting of two eternities, the past and future, is precisely the present moment—as Thoreau once quipped—then I present to you the game, basketball, that you may have forgotten.

Noting that on January 17, 2011, it will have been a half century since the greatest assembly ever to grace a hardwood floor and play basketball did so right here in Central New York, I want you to mark your calendar. Write to your local representative and don't ask, but demand, that a sign be erected outside the Onondaga War Memorial that might read: "On January 17, 1961, 20 percent of the greatest athletes to ever play the game of basketball did so right here. From Oscar Robertson, Jerry West and Wilt Chamberlain to Bob Cousy, Dolph Schayes and Bill Russell, the very best to ever a play a sport—and a game this community so dearly loves—did so for our benefit and in our hometown."

ACKNOWLEDGEMENTS

The day my grandchildren come to me and ask me about the game of basketball in Syracuse, New York, I want to pick them up, place them on my knee and dance with their imaginations through a book that although restricted in space and imagery—a matter of pure economics—was unobstructed by passion. We'll open a new pack of trading cards, flip them over, "stats side up," and compare figures, knowing that a foul shot, regardless of when it was made, was still worth only a point. We'll marvel at accounts, images and statistics from names we have forgotten or never knew to begin with. The players we'll visit will become just as real and just as important as anyone currently playing the game. I selfishly want another generation to appreciate my heroes, the great men in this book.

I would like to pass along my gratitude to The History Press: Catherine Clegg, Julie Foster and her editorial/production team (especially Ryan Finn), Amelia Lacey, Dani McGrath, Katie Parry, Brittain Phillips, Lara Simpson, Whitney Tarella and Saunders Robinson.

I would like to extend my appreciation to the following individuals: Ed Dahler, Harry Gallatin, Bob Houbregs, Bailey Howell, Edward Kalafat, Bill Kenville, Bob Kurland, Clyde Lovellette, Slater Martin, James E. Neal, Wally Osterkorn, the late Red Parton, Arnie Risen, Dolph Schayes and Bill Sharman. I also contacted many family members; some contributed, others could not. Nevertheless, I am grateful. Also, to our neighbors and friends who still have stories to tell, including "the Last Nationals Fan" (who chooses to remain anonymous), Ben DiFrancisco, Michael DiRenzio, Jeffrey

Gleason, John Kerrigan, Bill Martin, Ann Meyer, Jack Nelson, Anthony Rossi and Ross Stagnitti.

To write a book about hoops, you must jump through them, and this involves many, many people and numerous organizations. I am grateful to the following for their cooperation: Getty Images and Peter Berenc—thank you for the wonderful images and all your help; Elizabeth Baker; the Library of Congress and its outstanding staff; the National Basketball Association, especially the Philadelphia 76ers and the Oklahoma City Thunder; the Naismith Memorial Basketball Hall of Fame in Springfield, Massachusetts, and its great staff, especially Matt Zeyswing and Kip Fonsh—thank you for all of your time and hard work; LeMoyne College, home to the Daniel Biasone Archive; Syracuse University—Jim Boeheim, head coach, men's basketball, and Pete Moore, director of athletic communications; and Jeff Morey. Also, Barristers Herb Cohen and David Weinstein.

Every Syracuse hoops fan owes a debt of gratitude to those who have kept professional basketball alive for decades, including the writers and columnists, many from the Syracuse newspapers (Bill Reddy, L.J. Skiddy, Sean Kirst, Bud Poliquin and others); broadcast journalists (radio and television—Marv Albert, Len Berman, Bob Costas Marty Glickman and many more); local sports organizations; and the players.

From hosting a local reception for the movie *Blue Chips* and presenting Jim Boeheim's radio show to even sharing a 2005 *Sports Illustrated* article with the finest basketball writer ever, Jack McCallum, I have had the great pleasure to interact with numerous individuals in and around the sport of basketball. Many have been a source of inspiration for this book, especially the late Paul Seymour Sr. Thank you!

My passion for the game is primarily due to a father, Ford William Baker, who could play and did so well for North High and Broome Tech, in Binghamton, New York. I love you, Dad!

My heartfelt appreciation also extends to my incredible father-in-law, Richard Long, patriarch of a Long family (sorry I missed Iceland); to Aaron, Elizabeth and Rebecca, whom I will always assist; and to my wonderful wife, Alison Long, whom I will always guard with my affection.

Introduction

A NATIONALS MEDLEY

People, Places and Things

By "The Last Nationals Fan."

If my memory serves me well—and it may not, because they say a clear conscience is usually the sign of a bad memory—then I may be the last Nationals fan, and that worries me. You see, I do not want to be the Millvina Dean of the Syracuse hardwood. Not that I wouldn't be proud, mind you; I just wouldn't want the pressure of having to get the story right time after time after time. I still can't figure out why my memory is good enough to retain the insignificance that happens to me and yet not good enough to recollect how often I have told it to the same person. And that also bothers me.

In the fall of 2013, it will have been fifty years since the Syracuse Nationals left town. While grateful for the longevity, their departure still hurts—but not nearly as bad as knowing that I may not outlive the last Celtics fan. As memories fade, days are often reduced to only moments or a simple cherished name, but both can still evoke an emotion—if they can be recalled. Without further elaboration, in fact very little, here are my Nats memories or word associations. You fill in the gaps—like Seymour in a charging lane.

PEOPLE

I am not sure if it was Johnny Kerr or Robert Byrne who said, "There are two kinds of people, those who finish what they start and so on"…Forest "Frosty" Able, a single game of two shots…"Fall back, baby" Barnett, oh that shot… Danny Biasone, short, even with the hat, and his adorable accent…Nat "Feets" Broudy, a longtime basketball timekeeper at Madison Square Garden and Bill Bradley's personal towel keeper…Carmen Basilio, the boxer… Basilio "Buz" Cua, the musician…Mike Dempsey, Syracuse sign painter turned sports fanatic…Jack Dugger, playing football for the Buffalo Bisons… Bill "The Bullet" Gabor's, Duty, Honor and Country; thirty months' service during World War II, now that's a hero…Hal Greer, punctual, but don't talk to him in the morning…Johnny Kerr's comedy routines…Al Masino officiating Syracuse University games or running basketball camps with Al Cervi in Rochester…Jim McKechnie, his colorful WNDR broadcasts [the Nationals' road games were broadcast by ticker tape, which was sent from the visitors' court to the WNDR studios over a phone line]…Bill McCahan, his baseball career and "no-hitter" against the Washington Senators…Frank Selvy, "The Corbin Comet"…Don Savage, a LeMoyne Dolphin graduate who didn't have far to swim…Connie Simmons, straight from Flushing High School…Lawrence J. "Skid(s)" Skiddy, sports editor, *Herald-Journal*, had more rhetoric than Runyon…Art Van Auken's friendly smile…Mr. and Mrs. Woody Williams, of 312 Highland Avenue, always extending a helping hand…George Yardley's lightning-fast release…Lou Zara, Nationals business manager and publicity director, "Let me show ya somethin"…Red Auerbach, who may have crooned, "Pick your battles, those big enough to matter, but small enough to win"…Classic Syracuse Confrontations: Biasone v. (Les) Harrison, Al Cervi v. LeRoy Chollet, two Buffalo Boys (okay, "hardheads") who never backed down, Cervi v. (Les) Harrison, Cervi v. Charlie Eckman, a contrast, to put it mildly, Cousy v. "The Syracuse Flu," still won't admit to it, Seymour v. Auerbach, the famous "Egg Game of 1961," both were shelled, and William "Pop" Gates v. Chick Meehan, a classic confrontation (1946–47).

PLACES

A rookie once told the Nats' team doctor, "I broke my leg in two places." He told him to quit going to those places…the Hancock Airport tarmac, where Biasone often greeted the team plane…the Club Office, 120 East

Fayette Street, Tel. 3-7331...Eastwood Barber Shop, tell Nick to cut it short...Garzone's South Side restaurant and nightclub; "Hey, is that Dolph?"...Lakeshore Country Club, Danny Biasone member...McCarthy's Restaurant, the Only Original Oyster Bar in Syracuse, 1026 South Salina Street..."Old Syracuse Room" at the Jefferson-Clinton Hotel...the Hotel Onondaga Travel Bar, serving a noonday winner: beef sandwich for forty-five cents...Saturday Salina Street walks...room number seven inside the Boston Garden...Vocational High School where Biasone also played interscholastic golf...waiting inside the Erie Boulevard train station...the Yates, opposite city hall, single $1.50 up, double $2.50 up...the Player's Lounge inside the War Memorial, "Wish me luck honey!"... the Eastwood Sports Center (ESC) opens in 1941...the charming smiles of Danny and Rachel...Danny and Leo (Ferris) booth banter...great food; pass the ketchup Johnny... where's Elva?...no, it was Johnny who put sugar in the saltshaker...meeting at the ESC for road trips...breakfast before practice...an informal Eastwood playground encounter with an NBA player...ESC, "Where Good Fellows Get Together," seating capacity: 125, Tel 3-9939...Bowling Alley 2-8936... the demolition of the ESC in November 1999.

THINGS

Nothing in Syracuse is impossible, just less likely...Al Bianchi's stories about rooming with Johnny Kerr...Danny's Borsalino hats...Rachel Biasone laundering player uniforms...Cervi's lineup speeches..."aaand Cervi"...Cervi's trademark gesticulations..."Bangboards boys! Hit those bangboards!"...smoke clouds over the Coliseum floor...Al Cervi coaching the Lakers?...Cervi and the 1945–46 NBL Champion Rochester Royals, his favorite team...Cervi's three greatest players (1948): George Mikan, Bobby McDermott and Jim Pollard...a championship share of $1,100 (although the figure continues to change over the years) and a silver ice bucket...Congress Beer, Quinn's Beer and Panda Lager...Larry Costello playing all but twenty seconds during a six-overtime Niagara victory over Siena...boy, these college boys remember every detail...Joe Charles "Popular Player Contest" for a twenty-five-dollar victory bond...dead spots on the parquet floor at the Boston Garden...dressing in a car due to time restraints...gamblers in the Armory...halftime light changes inside the Coliseum..."Where's Swede?"...intermission periods livened up by Hammond organist Peg Kimball, a local theater favorite, with vocals by

WNDR baritone Bud Sova...Johnny Kerr's Christmas parties...Lucky "A" Awards included $5.00 gift certificate to Norene Dress Shop and even a dozen roses from John Lamanna Florist...meal money, five to seven dollars a day...one-year contracts...doesn't Chick Meehan resemble a tall Bob Hope?...the pin ladies sitting in the front row of the War Memorial... is that Ed Peterson yelling?..."Pour it on"...Red Rocha stories about Hawaii, Slats Gill and the "Thrill Kids"...Referee Ralph Fowler getting punched by the diminutive Jerry Rizzo, as the Denver Nuggets beat Syracuse 60–54 (1948–49)...shaking the Coliseum bangboards..."The Strangler" prowling around the visitors' bench, always made Cousy nervous...an all-night championship victory party at the home of Bob Sexton..."The Strangler" dancing on the game seven championship floor with Paul Seymour...Schayes's recollections of the St. Louis Browns...the NBA's 25th Anniversary All-Time Team in 1970 and its 50th Anniversary All-Time Team in 1996..."Adolph Schayles," aka Dolph Schayes, as it appeared in a Syracuse program during the 1949–50 season...train trips, oh, the train trips, card games, deli sandwiches late at night...the Empire State to New York City...we really wore those uniforms...a practice of five colored uniform starters versus five white shirts...plays first fellas, then scrimmage...George Yardley and his national age group tennis doubles titles...and finally, a championship banner raising (next to Carmen's) on February 1, 1997, inside the Onondaga County War Memorial.

God, we miss you boys!

PART I
A Prelude

Chapter 1

BASKET BALL

S o distinct a sound that it is instantly identifiable—combined with an echo from an empty gymnasium, or Armory, it can be as haunting as it is rhythmic, like the beating of our heart. It is potential energy in our hands, until it falls, when extra energy is released as a result of its motion. It creates that sound—*tant, tant, tant*. Sound energy transferred, awaiting deposit. The moment the basketball strikes the gloss of the exterior hardwood, potential energy becomes zero and the object bounces until it is stopped by our hand. Of the four major American sports—three of which use a ball—its resonance is the most recollected, instant memories. Unleashed into the control of a superior athlete, this power is daunting. But when "basket ball" was invented, it was *not* basketball as you know it today.

As a London welfare movement that began in 1844, the YMCA (Young Men's Christian Association) was a hostel or recreational facility run by the organization. Quickly expanding worldwide, the concept promoted moral correctness in sports activities, both indoors and out. It was an admirable goal, focused on all four seasons.

However, winter months, like those experienced in Central New York, were not conducive to the popular outdoor sports of the time—baseball and football—so alternatives to calisthenics and gymnastics needed to be considered. And contemplated they were, as the call for a new competitive game to be played indoors was made and answered by Dr. James Naismith.

During the winter of 1891, Naismith, an instructor at the International YMCA Training School in Springfield, Massachusetts, conceived of an

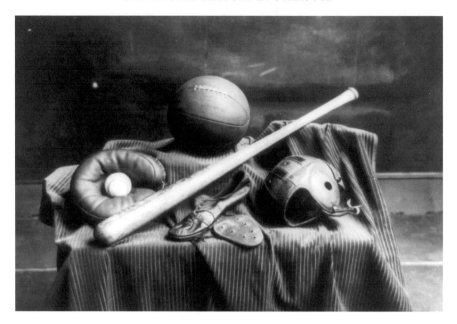

Dr. Naismith's gift of "basket ball" is played in more than two hundred countries around the world. *Library of Congress LC-USZ62-96727.*

activity favorable to wooden floors and artificial light (prerequisites). It must be an interesting activity, he thought, easy to learn and even a bit similar to other popular sports. The subject of the activity was a ball—a successful control vehicle used in other sports—to allow for movement; after all, this was a friendly, noncontact sport, where running was not allowed. A sport where the majority of play, so Naismith believed, would take place above the player's head. Precision would be emphasized over power, as scoring, or direct contact between the ball and a container, became the desired objective. When two peach baskets were nailed overhead—a common gymnasium feature during this era was an overhead track balcony—the name "basketball" was derived.

Thirteen simple rules guided Naismith's sport—a majority of which are still in use today—promoting agility, movement, speed and, of course, teamwork; it would be a game where accuracy would determine outcome. The expedient dissemination of the game was enhanced by the organizational skills of the YMCA—the perfect conduit. Instructors delighted in teaching area youth the fundamentals of the game at places such as the Alhambra, a multidimensional facility in Syracuse. When the venue, located at 275 James Street, wasn't hosting roller skating or a boxing match, "cagers" were

Basket Ball

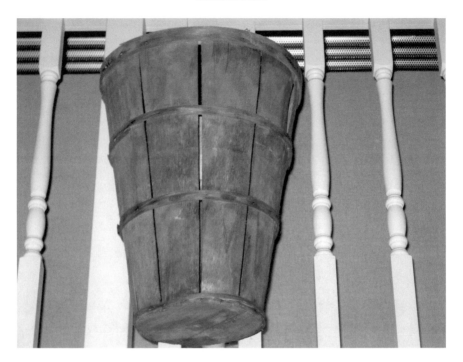

The simplicity of a peach basket, a ball and a gifted educator provides the world with "a new game." *Naismith Memorial Basketball Hall of Fame.*

welcomed to refine their skills. Other institutions also expressed interest in the activity; some Central New York residents learned of the game when it was introduced during an 1892 gym class at Cornell University. This institute of higher learning used these classes to create basketball disciples—hardwood acolytes, if you will. Similarly, Yale—a future Ivy League participant located in New Haven, Connecticut—was the first university to put a basketball team on the road, but others quickly followed. The popularity of the new indoor activity soared, and it wasn't long before the emergence of semiprofessional teams, as opportunists conceptualized "dollar signs over dribbles."

The acceptance of the game also bred innovation, with the open metal basket one of the first alterations approved in 1906. No longer did someone—often a person positioned in the track balcony—have to retrieve the ball after a basket. But popularity also bred contempt, often in the form of overzealous spectators—some even took the game into their own hands by preventing the ball from entering the creel. Thus backboards were introduced, first wire (1893) and wood (1904), later glass (1909), then wood again and then (fiber-) glass.

Dr. James Naismith (1861–1939) was foremost an educator, dedicated to developing character through sports and recreation. This statue appears inside the Naismith Memorial Basketball Hall of Fame.

Boundaries, initially imaginary, were enhanced by rails (in New England), high-wire cages (eleven feet) or nets (on all four sides)—particularly around courts used by professionals. While many independent teams shunned the cages, the first professional league (National Basketball League, 1898) made use mandatory during its games held in Pennsylvania or New Jersey. With the ball never leaving the playing area, both the fans and the game could be contained; backboards were no longer needed. Thus the term "cagers" became synonymous with basketball players—initially affectionately applied but later enhanced by the animal demeanor exhibited inside the confine. Now resting at the end of a support, the basket was home to the perfect shot, be it via simple layups, static fouls or long attempts. By 1903, a rectangular court, with painted lines, became acceptable at a variety of sizes; after all, it was Oscar Wilde, a cager of a different sort, who said, "Consistency is the last refuge of the unimaginative."

A basketball team officially consisted of five men, although variations have been tried over the years—for example, larger gyms occasionally opted for nine (Naismith's original recommendation). The players used a soccer ball at first before a standard leather ball was accepted (developed by A.G. Spalding in 1894). The (NBA) sphere, which is now 29.5 inches in circumference and weighs twenty-two ounces, has undergone numerous surface alterations.

The YMCA joined forces with the AAU (Amateur Athletic Union) in 1894. Game information was enhanced by the printing of the first "official guide" by the Spalding Company—a sporting goods company run by former baseball player and gifted entrepreneur A.G. Spalding. The NCAA (National Collegiate Athletic Association) joined forces with the AAU in 1915 to form the Joint Basketball Rules Committee; it existed until 1933. The rules became standardized, and by 1950, as fate might have it, one hundred more statutes had been added to Naismith's original thirteen; these guidelines were more advanced for professionals.

Significant rule changes over the years have included the elimination of the initially acceptable double dribble and the requiring of a center jump after each foul. Modifications were also made to allow a player who is dribbling to shoot before passing, which was a former requirement, and to allow a player to shoot his own fouls rather than a team specialist. Time restrictions were also added: a rule was applied to prevent a team from keeping possession of the ball in the defensive end for longer than ten seconds, and an offensive player was not allowed to remain in the foul lane, with or without the ball, for longer than three seconds. All of these rules, and a few others, were meant to improve the game, and they worked.

Level of proficiency also evolved, albeit at different rates. While the game became popular at many colleges, there was little interaction between schools before the mid-1930s. Finally, when a good rivalry did take place, it was often at a complex far too small to accommodate fans; it was Wilde again who quipped, "Everything popular is wrong." Enter sportswriter turned promoter Ned Irish, born in Lake George, New York, who understood the value of a venue. On December 29, 1934, he scheduled the first double-header at Madison Square Garden, featuring New York University versus Notre Dame (score, 25–18) and Westminster versus St. John's University (score, 37–33). A throng of 16,180 fans was a testament to his efforts and verification to many of the game's acceptance.

But similar to the evolution of other popular sports, issues soon surfaced that hampered the game, including biased referees and timekeepers provided by home teams, players jumping teams or playing for multiple squads and even multiple organization ownership. If the game was going to thrive, all of these concerns had to be rectified—problems that could be corrected, so most people thought, by the proper individuals under a structured organization.

Early professional leagues—and there were many, some using the same name—also took root before 1950, beginning with the National Basketball League, 1898–1903. Names worth noting for Central New Yorkers, due to proximity and participation, would include the Hudson River League, 1909–12; the New York State League, 1911–23; the Interstate League, 1915–17, 1919–20; the Metropolitan Basketball League, 1921–28, 1931–33; the American Basketball League, 1925–31, 1933–45; the National Basketball League, 1926–27; the National Basketball League, 1929–30; the National Basketball League, 1932–33; the Midwest Basketball Conference, 1935–37; the National Basketball League, 1937–49; the Basketball Association of America, 1946–49; the Professional Basketball League of America, 1947–48; and the National Basketball Association, 1949–present.

A few early characters emerged—including Joe Fogarty, set shot ace Harry Hough, defensive genius Winnie Kinkade, "Banty" Marshall, passer Roy Steele, Andy Suils and John Wendelken—but they received little attention for their prowess. Team distinction was paramount—after all, this was a game conceived from Christian values.

Now to quote Wilde, for the last time: "The only thing worse than being talked about is not being talked about." I would be remiss not to comment about origin. The genesis of professional basketball is believed to have been in Trenton, New Jersey; however, if you live in Central New York, you may find yourself supporting claims that Herkimer, New York, deserves further consideration (see "Speculation Regarding the First Professional Game" on page 30). Remember, basketball was in its infancy, popular in YMCAs and a few other organizations but certainly not in the public eye like other sports. It is therefore conceivable that other professional teams existed but were not publicly acknowledged. Since it is certain that members of the Trenton Basketball Team received payment for their services during the 1896–97 season, and that earlier claims remain unsubstantiated, us "Upstaters" must reluctantly acknowledge the Garden State.

THE GREAT TEAMS EMERGE

With at least one salaried league in operation from 1900 to World War I, there was professional basketball, even if the organizations were confined to the Northeast and typically unstable. In contrast to league play, independent teams, such as the Buffalo Germans, flourished by facing YMCAs, college teams, semipro clubs and assorted other varieties. Thanks to barnstorming trips, league play may have been an option but certainly not a necessity.

Enhanced by media accounts the art of barnstorming was perhaps at its pinnacle in the mid-1920s. Sports teams, particularly prominent ones, or well-known individuals such as baseball players like Lou Gehrig or Babe Ruth and even the boxer Jack Dempsey, would occasionally travel to various locations, usually small towns, to stage exhibition matches. The art of touring in this manner was known as "barnstorming" since performances were often held in barns—frequently the largest facility in a small town.

The reason for the action was simple: money. Yes, barnstorming could attract new fans to a sport and sell a few souvenirs, but underlying everything was financial gain. While barnstorming teams lacking a home arena did so out of necessity, other teams merely did it as a way to generate revenue during the off-season. It was an element outside of a formal organization, running parallel to the sport, equally as exciting and certainly evolutionary (see "Harlem Globetrotters, 1927–Present" on page 31).

Like any team sport, greatness emerged, a ramification of factors such as performance, precision, proximity and even circumstance. Since the best play often meant the best pay, players were drawn to winning teams. With league play in its infancy, barnstorming teams represented the premier opportunities. Five such teams were the first to capture the hearts of residents of the Empire State.

The German Team of Buffalo, New York, 1895–1925

They won the 1901 Pan American Exposition (PAE) Championship in Buffalo and the 1904 Olympic exhibition title in St. Louis, went undefeated in five of their first eighteen seasons and even posted more than 100 straight victories—not bad for six youths with very humble beginnings. Organized as a boys' team in 1895 at a YMCA on Buffalo's East Side, the independent German team found their way to the championship of Western New York. Playing some of the finest basketball of the day, winning for them became commonplace against both professional and amateur teams. In a testament to their skill, the Germans even defeated Hobart College, 134–0. In 1908, led by star player Al Heerdt and coach Fred Burkhardt, the team won 111 straight games (1908–1910). When the legendary boys disbanded in 1925, they had compiled an impressive 792-86 record. Later, the group became one of only five teams enshrined in the Basketball Hall of Fame (1961).

Of note, when the AAU held its 1901 all-around championships at the PAE (outdoors), it included a basketball tournament. Eight of the teams, including the Germans, were from the Northeast: St. Joseph's Literary Institute of Cambridge (Massachusetts); the Entre Nous Athletic Club (Paterson, New Jersey, later the Paterson Crescents); St. Joseph's (Paterson, New Jersey); the Institute Athletic Club of Newark (New Jersey); the National Athletic Club of Brooklyn (New York); the 17th Separate Company of Flushing (New York); and a small school familiar perhaps to some of you, St. John's School of Manlius (Central New York, Onondaga County).

The Original Celtics of New York, 1914–1941

The Celtics, as an idea originating from Frank McCormack, were compiled from teenage boys living on Manhattan's West Side in 1914. They stressed fundamental skills, determination and solid team play. When the team was

The 1925 Original Celtics visit the White House. The team featured players like Dutch Dennert, Nat Holman, John Beckman and Joe Lapchick. *Library of Congress, LC-DIG-npcc-13023.*

re-formed following World War I—a time when basketball was certainly not a prime concern—promoters James and Tom Furey continued where McCormack had left off. Renaming them "The Original Celtics," the club set forth to set a new basketball performance standard. The Furey brothers had the foresight and vision to bring the game into larger arenas, which they did by moving it into the 71st Regiment Armory, the second-biggest arena in New York. Later, the Celtics became so popular that they could draw ten thousand fans per night for a game at their new home, Madison Square Garden.

The squad featured several Hall of Famers, including pivot play forward Dutch Dennert, outstanding passer Nat Holman, playmaker John Beckman and dominant center Joe Lapchick. Primarily barnstormers, the club spent all or part of four seasons in leagues picking up a few distinctions along the way, including ABL Championships in 1926 and 1927. While bringing the game a style and a pace more conducive to attracting fans, the Celtics are also credited with many innovations, including the post play, zone defenses and switching man-to-man protection. They even set the stage for team-player negotiation as the first professional organization to sign exclusive player contracts.

31st SEPARATE COMPANY OF HERKIMER, NEW YORK

Frank Basloe was born in Budapest, Hungary, and immigrated to the United States at an early age. Settling in New York State's scenic Mohawk Valley, in the hamlet of Herkimer, he took an interest in a game that was garnering significant local attention: "basket ball." Witnessing local YMCA director Lambert G. Will promoting the sport, or a variety of it, Basloe became intrigued with the possibilities—so much so that by the age of sixteen (1903) he was organizing his first professional team. From this point forward, minus an interval occupied by World War I, Basloe's teams barnstormed throughout New England and the mid-Atlantic region. His most successful team went by the name the 31st Separate Company of Herkimer, also known—with modest variation—as the Oswego Indians and Basloe's Globe Trotters.

The highlight of this period, and perhaps one of basketball's greatest games, was when the 31st Separate Company defeated the Buffalo Germans (either 26–21 or 18–16 depending on the account) in front of 2,800 fans at the Mohawk Armory in February 1911. The victory snapped the legendary team's 111-game winning streak.

The Mohawk Armory in Mohawk, New York, was home to many historic games of "basket ball" under the watchful eye of Frank Basloe.

Certainly one of basketball's premier impresarios at the time, Basloe's teams took on all comers. They continued to play the Germans and others throughout the area, in places like Oswego and Tonawanda, before heading to the Midwest.

Speculation Regarding the First Professional Game

Basloe also promoted—and in 1952 even penned—the theory that basketball, which clearly had some deep roots in Upstate New York, played its first professional game in Herkimer. Taking place during the frosty first months of 1893, a rugby ball–stimulated activity entertained more than 150 spectators at the Fox Opera House. Because the Herkimer team, one of the game's participants, received a gate payment, Basloe asserted that this was the first professional game. While this claim is intriguing, it remains controversial with historians to this day.

New York Renaissance, 1922–1949

The all-black New York Renaissance mastered the art of precision and illusory ball handling. From their founding by Hall of Famer Robert L. Douglas in 1922 to their disbanding in 1949, the Rens barnstormed throughout the country, routing their antagonists while establishing themselves as one of basketball's first true dynasties.

Named for Harlem's Renaissance Casino—the second-story ballroom serving as their home court and a facility they rarely played in—the Rens drew attention to the uptown borough. Since no existing pro league would accept a black team into its ranks, the team was forced to barnstorm. In retrospect, the methodology eroded racial barriers and contributed greatly to their popularity and that of the game.

Despite all obstacles the Rens won more than two thousand games; in one amazing eighty-six-day stretch during the 1932–33 season, the Rens won eighty-eight straight games. Other career highlights include capturing the World Professional Tournament in 1939, dominating their competition over a twenty-five-year span and introducing everyone to Hall of Famers William "Pop" Gates and Charles "Tarzan" Cooper.

Harlem Globetrotters, 1927–Present

Synonymous with the game of "basket ball," perhaps more than any other organization, the world-famous Harlem Globetrotters propelled the game to a new threshold. From their humble South Side of Chicago beginnings—many players originating out of Wendell Phillips High School and playing for "Giles Post" before joining the Savoy Big Five under manager Dick Hudson—this organization has risen to worldwide prominence.

It was impresario, and future Hall of Famer, Abe Saperstein who later bought the team and renamed it the Harlem Globetrotters. People often forget that the Globetrotters were a serious competitive team until the late 1930s, and in 1940 they won the prestigious World Professional Basketball Tournament in Chicago.

The Globetrotters began blending light entertainment and comedic routines into their appearances with the addition of Inman Jackson in 1939. "Big Jack" was the first big man added to the act—although he was only six foot three—and the key ingredient to bond his team together. The "globetrotting image" emerged following World War II, when the team increased their international travel; they have played in more than twenty thousand games in over one hundred countries around the world. A noted highlight, part of the group's twenty-fifth anniversary tour (1951) was a game before seventy-five thousand fans in Berlin's Olympic Stadium.

The following year, "Sweet Georgia Brown" became the team's signature song and a melody instantly identifiable with them. With players such as Geese Ausbie, Marques Haynes, Meadowlark Lemon, Curly Neal and Goose Tatum, the Globetrotters became basketball's ambassadors, bringing their showmanship and goodwill to millions while embellishing part of basketball's storied history.

NEW YORK STATE LEAGUE, 1911–1917, 1919–1923

In addition to the barnstorming teams that frequented Upstate New York, the most visible teams a century ago were those in the organized New York State League. They included Adams, Massachusetts; Amsterdam, Catskills–Albany (Senators); Cohoes; Gloversville; Hudson; Kingston (Colonials); Mohawk (Indians); Newburgh-Syracuse; Paterson, New Jersey (Crescents); Pittsfield, Massachusetts; Poughkeepsie-Brooklyn (Dodgers); Saratoga–Glens Falls; Schenectady-Kingston; Troy (Trojans); and Utica (Utes). All of the teams in the league played in armories, had cages or netting and did not use backboards. It was a rough game, with extensive blocking and overlooked fouls—not for the faint of heart. It was also a dynamic sport, where every year the players seemed to get taller and stronger—a player near or at six and a half feet tall was considered a giant.

Transferring to Syracuse during the 1913–14 campaign, the Newburgh team tried but failed to generate sufficient local interest to sustain the club—they dropped out by the end of the season.

STATE ARMORY ACTION: SYRACUSE

Prompted by Birney P. Lynch, then a sports editor at the *Post-Standard* newspaper, a couple "Hill Cagers," Joe Schwarzer (1916–18, Syracuse letterman) and Wilbur Crisp (1914–17), gathered some friends for local contests in 1919. For several years both—along with Bill Rafter (1915–17), Jim Casey (1916–17), local boy Jim Tormery (Georgetown), Howie Ortner

(Cornell) and others—packed them into the state Armory on Jefferson Street. Engaging the best teams they could find, which wasn't always easy, it was a promising prophecy of hoops and wood.

THE ALL-AMERICANS

At Syracuse University, from 1923 to 1927, if there was a major sport being played, it was likely that Victor A. Hanson was participating—he captained baseball, basketball and football. Born on July 30, 1903, the Watertown, New York native seemed to live for competition. Becoming synonymous with the idea of an all-American, Hanson would take the distinction, along with his athletic prowess, into professional sports, playing for the Cleveland Rosenblums in the American Basketball League before creating his own team in Syracuse (All-Americans, also called Hanson's Syracusans and Hanson's All-Syracuse team).

Vic Hanson brought his "cagers" to play inside the State Armory, located a few blocks from Clinton Square in Syracuse.

The city welcomed its favorite son back inside the Jefferson Street Armory in January 1928. Hanson, as expected, brought some talented cagers with him, including Harlan "Gotch" Carr (1925) and Charlie Lee (1925–27). As fans acquainted themselves with names like Brounstein, Conway, Follette, Cimpi and Roach, they could also enjoy music both at halftime and after the game by the Wainwrights; Hanson was also no stranger to textbook marketing, and neither was his business associate, Harry Markowitz.

Their local adversaries included independent teams from Rochester (Jack Newmann's Oldsmobile Five), Geneva (All-Stars), Elmira (Eclipse Five), Schenectady (Professionals) and Utica (Dewey Steffan's All-Utica Five). Teams such as Jim Thorpe's Indian team, the (New York) Whirlwind Five and Renaissance Five also tackled with Hanson's basketeers. Rivalries also presented themselves, such as Hanson's battle against former Union college graduate (1926) "Sig" Makofski—both players had been hailed in the press as the greatest college basketball players.

On January 21, 1928, a crowd of more than two thousand took to the Armory to watch Hanson, Brounstein, Lee, Carr and Roach tackle an all-star lineup from New York that included McCrystal, Povey, Knoblock, Bowden and Eggert. The 34–21 victory by Hanson and crew was far from a delicate affair, as fouls were disregarded as a means for expulsion. The terms and conditions were worked out in advance between Hanson and another all-star squad member by the name of Lou Gehrig. Hanson, who had also agreed to play baseball with the New York Yankees organization, would reunite with his friend during spring training. (The Syracuse All-Americans were part of the ABL, 1929–30, but did not finish the season.)

In 1930, Hanson gave up professional basketball to become the head coach of football at Syracuse University. Markowitz and Asher Markson kept the venture going for a couple years and then stepped aside.

SYRACUSE REDS

From 1939 to 1941, the Syracuse Reds were a popular attraction both as an independent basketball club and as brief members of Frank J. Basloe's organization. (Due to financial needs, teams would also book games with sovereign groups, a contentious issue with Basloe.) Tackling many of the popular barnstorming teams of the day, like the Original Celtics basketball club or the New York Renaissance, along with league foes meant competitive basketball at its finest.

While not shy to engage a local team—such as the Baldwinsville High School alumni cagers—in an exhibition the Reds preferred the challenge of familiar faces, such as the 1939–40 Newark Elks, who included center Edgar Sonderman (1935–37) and Lloyd "Skids" Sanford (1933–35), two former Syracuse varsity lettermen, and Tom Rich, former Cornell University captain.

Drawing from local talent, the Reds included Syracuse standouts Wilmeth Sidat-Singh (1937–39), who was selected as team captain; Mark Haller (1938–39); future Nats coach Al Cervi; and Christian Brothers Academy's Bob Nugent (CBA is a private Catholic college preparatory school in suburban Syracuse, New York). Other players included John Bromberg, player-manager Jake Costello, captain Clarkson Tech, Dave Paris, Bud Clancy, Bob Stewart (1937–39) and John Schroeder, just to name a select few.

Obtaining a facility, such as the Jefferson Street Armory, for pro basketball wasn't always easy, as a state National Guard order required that the drillsheds be kept available for drilling. Scheduling games was often limited to Wednesday or Saturday nights, with others thrown in when available. Fan interest was always a concern, so it wasn't unusual to complement games with other attractions. For example, a preliminary game between the Rochester Filarets, national girls' champions, might be added.

The Reds became so accomplished that they were invited to the 1940 World Professional Basketball Tournament; making it into the semifinal round, they were defeated by the Harlem Globetrotters 34–25. (It's worth noting that Sidat-Singh and Stewart played for Rochester in the WPBT.) Seven years later, the Syracuse Nationals, along with the Mohawk Redskins (Herkimer, New York), were also invited to the WPBT—the last Upstate New York teams to attend. (Neither team made it past the first round.)

With change a part of the evolutionary process, the 1940–41 season witnessed the Reds with a new coach, Vic Hanson (who was replaced as head football coach at Syracuse University in 1937 by Oscar "Ossie" Solem), and playing in a new facility, the State Fair Coliseum. The Reds were also without a familiar face, Wilmeth Sidat-Singh, who had joined the Renaissance Five of New York City (1940). Having returned home to Washington, D.C., after graduation, Singh also barnstormed with the Washington Bruins/Lichtman Bears.

Wilmeth Sidat-Singh signed on with the armed forces in August 1942, graduated from flight school in March 1943 and was assigned to the segregated armed forces' only pilot training program for African Americans, the 332nd (the Tuskegee Airmen). While on a training mission, the engine of his plane failed over Lake Huron and he died; he is buried at Arlington National Cemetery.

During the war years of 1942 to 1945, there were priorities, and basketball wasn't one.

THE EARLY GAME: A BRIEF TIME-OUT

As the game evolved, the guard position was used for more than defense, the center (the team's tallest person) for more than the "tap" play and the forward for more than shooting and running. Every player on a team had to learn to run, pass, dribble and shoot.

Offense

Basketball emerged as a game of movement, impressing fans with its speed, fast cutting, passing, dribbling and motion. The most familiar directive by a 1950s basketball coach was likely "Don't stand still!" But others quickly followed, including to stay low and keep busy offensively, to not run in a straight line and vary your movement, to keep the scoring lanes open and avoid standing pivots unless you are screening and to master the fake (if you have the ball, take the long first step and then dribble with the away hand). Do all of this while keeping your eyes on your man and knowing the location of the ball.

Since the primary purpose of the game is to outscore your opponent, a team had to learn how to advance the ball, either through passing or dribbling. Passing options, and there were many, included everything from the hook pass and one-handed overhead pass to the underhand flip and over-the-shoulder pass. All needed to be crisp and accurate. Dribbling emerged as an art, requiring uncanny control, with behind-the-back maneuvers and the ability to alternate hands. Combined with changing pace and effective deception, a good dribbler could have an enormous impact on an outcome.

Since it's not the number of shots you take that is important but rather the percentage you make, it didn't take long for teams to figure which ones those were. What were the high-percentage shots? Typically they were found to be a layup or pivot shot in the vicinity of the basket and a two-handed overhead shot farther away. A layup is a one-handed shot—typically one that rebounds off the backboard—made near the basket. It is one of the game's fundamental shots. A pivot or "turnaround" shot is made from a movement in which the player holding the ball may move in any direction with one foot while keeping the other (the pivot foot) in contact with the floor. The two-handed overhead shot is almost self-defining and is typically made from a "set" or stationary position. Other successful shots include the two-handed chest, the one-handed (set or moving) and the hook.

Defense

Defense is the art of stopping a score, preventing everything above, legally. This is done through one primary encounter: man to man. A defensive man confronts the person with the ball, regardless of what type of formation.

Coaches of the early game professed wisdom still applicable to this day, including picking up your man, staying between your man and the basket, guarding the scoring area and the dribbler, maintaining proper spacing, employing proper stance and footwork, not falling for fakes or leaving your feet and always—I mean always—knowing where the ball is. Do all of these things while maintaining your proper position, and you may be able to call yourself a basketball player.

The Spalding team trophy awarded to the New York State League 1911–12 champion Troy team. *Naismith Memorial Basketball Hall of Fame.*

Trophy (bottom) awarded to Al Cervi as the best player on the 1937–38 Buffalo Bisons team. *Naismith Memorial Basketball Hall of Fame.*

Chapter 2
SYRACUSE NATIONALS,
1946–1949

The NBL Years

Autumn, always a reflective time period, felt particularly pertinent in 1945. World War II had just ended, our soldiers were returning and the transition back to peacetime had begun. The world seemed smaller now, and everything "back home" meant more, especially our freedom. Optimism was bountiful, complemented by a strong economy and the yearning for a better life. Finally, we could smile and mean it.

Professional baseball, not basketball, mesmerized Americans, particularly in the large cities, followed by a rare athletic alternative—a heavyweight fight or major college football game. After all, athletic association, nurtured through familiarity, can take generations. The action-packed nature of professional basketball, which would eventually meld nicely with technology, needed to remain patient.

Manufacturing touched many cities during the war, and Syracuse was no exception—from specialty metal to custom machinery, many businesses thrived throughout Onondaga County. Two of the "Big Three" automobile manufacturers, Chrysler and General Motors, established major operations in the area, as did the Carrier Corporation (Willis Carrier moved his headquarters here from New Jersey in the 1930s—now a Subsidiary of UTC) and Crouse-Hinds (now Cooper Industries—a diversified worldwide manufacturer of electrical products). The General Electric Corporation (Martin Marietta/Lockheed Martin) also had its main television manufacturing plant located at Electronics Park, an impressive complex located in Liverpool (a suburb of Syracuse). Here in Central New York, corporations knew that they could find hardworking and dedicated labor—a prerequisite to any successful business.

Retail also flourished, as those who enjoyed shopping often found solace downtown, along Salina Street—"a place to see and be seen." It was safe, clean and vibrant. Walking north along the thoroughfare, under the red and green canvas awnings, people would marvel at the vertical signs—Fleischmans, Howard, Bono—gracing buildings on both sides of the street. The shopping was convenient, and it had all the excitement of a big city. "We would drive up on weekends, from Binghamton," spoke a gentleman from Broome County. "The girls could shop, while the guys might catch a basketball game at the Armory. It was the place to be."

In 1950, Syracuse's population peaked at 221,000—and that was just fine with the many families raising "baby boomers," part of the 76 million Americans born during the post–World War II era. Ethnic groups had already established themselves in the city, particularly the German, Irish, Italian and Polish. African Americans, like many cultures who had lived in Syracuse since our founding fathers, also came to Central New York to escape *some* of the racism and bigotry they had experienced elsewhere. The key word here being *some*, as like in similar northern cities education and racial tolerance still needed improvement.

An ethnological reflection is the twenty-six neighborhoods that make up the city of Syracuse. Traditionally, Irish, Polish and Ukrainian Americans settled on its west side; Jewish Americans on its east side; German and Italian Americans on the north side; and African Americans on its south side. To many expatriates, including Danny Biasone, it was the perfect melting pot.

Biasone—born in Miglianico, Cheti, Italy, on February 22, 1909—immigrated to the United States on Christmas Day 1919. Like most who arrived at Ellis Island, he was mesmerized by the imagery and reflection of capitalism. He and his father then departed northwest, for Syracuse—a familiar name, "Siracusa" being the name of an Italian port on the eastern coast of Sicily, and a seemingly welcome location. His first employment, he would often recall, was not in salt production like many of his predecessors but rather as a caddy at an area golf course, Onondaga Country Club. The hardworking youth was determined to be not just any bag jockey but rather the very best—a character trait that would follow him the rest of his life.

Gifted in athletics, Biasone became a star football player during his high school days in Syracuse. Later, he would often credit his father, a conductor with the Syracuse Transit Lines, for his love of sports. As he got older, his instinctive drive and competitive nature would surface in exploits such as the Syracuse Bisons, an independent football team. Stripped of his players during World War II, Biasone then turned to a semipro basketball team instead—people often forget that individuals could exceed the height limit for military service. Creative or astute options can be a derivative of a crisis, a fact Biasone understood.

The epicenter for most of Biasone's creativity was the Eastwood Sports Center, a bowling alley and restaurant run by Danny and his brother Joe. For more than five decades, this facility would serve their neighbors. Danny's wife Rachel, whom many knew as one of the Gelormini sisters, also played an integral role at the location at 2912 James Street—the east side of the city. Since the Syracuse metro area receives more snow on average than any other large municipality in the United States, those who cater to indoor recreation stay busy during the winter months. Hardwood dreams, on an alley or a court, could come true in Eastwood.

Having booked a basketball game with the nearby Rochester Royals that was canceled not once but twice by team owner Lester Harrison, a frustrated Biasone was led to the National Basketball League (NBL). He and a group of associates contacted the organization in Chicago and secured a franchise for a reported $5,000. Now with his own team, justice, Biasone thought, could be served against the Royals on his court.

ANOTHER NEW LEAGUE: A PLETHORA OF PROBLEMS

Born out of the Midwest Basketball Conference in 1935, the NBL—which consisted of company teams, corporate-sponsored squads and teams owned and operated by businessmen and independents—was founded in 1937. Conference management felt that the name change, National Basketball League, would increase media exposure—or "marketing appeal" as they called it—an attempt to attract a larger audience, which is logical when you realize that the NBL was driven by three corporations—General Electric (Electrics), Firestone (Non-Skids) and Goodyear (Wingfoots)—which were driven by profit. Company teams often attracted better talent by providing employment for their players—"quid pro quo." Not offering the same level of financial security made it difficult for the independents to compete.

The NBL was also affected by schedule debacles. A team's itinerary, and the attention to it, was left to the discretion of each of the organizations. Determined by the home team, the length of games also varied—either four ten-minute quarters or three fifteen-minute periods. The lack of detail and uniformity was staggering; the game needed parity not only in personnel but in procedure as well. Despite the incongruence, the league lasted twelve years before merging with the then three-year-old Basketball Association of America (BAA, formed by the Arena Managers Association of America) in 1949.

By the time Biasone's group joined the league in 1946, the confrontational issues were being punctuated by team dominance. The first dynasty to emerge was the Oshkosh All-Stars. Led by the pivot presence of LeRoy "Cowboy" Edwards, the All-Stars appeared in the championship series for five consecutive years (the 1937–38 season to the 1941–42 season) and won two titles (1940–41 and 1941–42). The six-foot-five center would eventually become the second-highest scorer in league history and also led the NBL in scoring his first three years as a pro.

The Zollner Pistons of Fort Wayne soon challenged the All-Stars, the distinctive team moniker attributable to industrialist Fred Zollner, whose company made the engine component. A pioneer, possessor and prophet, Zollner was also the financial lifeblood of the league during some of its most difficult times. His role as emancipator gained him the respect of many—including Biasone, in whom he confided often, especially with regard to rule modifications. Fort Wayne was commanded by "the greatest long-distance shooter in the history of the game," veteran Bobby McDermott. Moving directly from high school ball on Long Island to the pro ranks, he possessed the perfect two-handed set shot. It was his accuracy that led the team to two league titles (1943–44 and 1944–45); the NBL would later name McDermott the greatest player in league history (1946).

The Pistons' biggest threat came from the Sheboygan Red Skins. Beginning in 1941, the season before Fort Wayne joined the NBL, Sheboygan appeared in five championship series in six seasons. They lost to Oshkosh in the 1940–41 finals and beat Fort Wayne for the title in 1942–43 but lost to them in 1943–44 and 1944–45. Sheboygan was swept in the 1945–46 finals by the league's newest member, a powerhouse team from Rochester and a team that boasted the likes of Hall of Famers Al Cervi, Bob Davies and Red Holzman.

THE 1946–47 SEASON: UNCAGED

"They are turning the animals loose in the Armory," spoke a Nationals fan—part of a handful of bibulous fans who departed the old Jefferson-Clinton Hotel. Now standing patiently outside—only a point guard toss to the Armory grounds—and putting on their overcoats and puffing their cigarettes, most were satisfied that their pregame ritual had satisfactorily prepared them for today's contest. During a forty-four-game season, the Syracuse Nationals would confront eleven NBL teams (season record with each opponent is indicated in parentheses): Anderson (3-1), Detroit (3-1), Oshkosh (3-1), Youngstown (3-1), Tri-Cities (2-2), Fort Wayne (2-2), Sheboygan (2-2), Chicago (1-3), Indianapolis (1-3), Toledo (1-3) and Rochester (0-4). For fifteen cents, a souvenir program, featuring the handsome cover image of former Fordham star Jerry Rizzo, could attach a familiar name with a face and a face with a team, a worthy investment to some but an excess to more.

The inaugural crusade saw the team's offensive attack commanded by the durable Rizzo. A veteran cager, he played with the Kingston team in the New York State League and with the Paterson, New Jersey club in the American League (1945–46). Rizzo led Syracuse with a 10-points-per-game (PPG) average—the only team player in double figures—while compiling 479 total points. The next-highest Nats scorer, Mike Novak, finished 100 points behind (379). But "Big Mike" (six foot nine), who was purchased

An outstanding guard and precision shot artist, Bennie Borgmann (1900–1978) was enshrined in Springfield in 1961. This display appears inside the Naismith Memorial Basketball Hall of Fame.

from Sheboygan for $5,000, took command of the pivot position for the team—exactly where they wanted him. An indestructible John Chaney, a standout at Louisiana State University, followed both of his teammates and averaged 8.6 PPG. Also contributing to the team's 53.3 average production mark were former St. Louis Blues star George Nelmark, former Red Skins defensive standout Steve Sharkey, CBA graduate John "Chick" Meehan and former Michigan University star John Gee—all found a median above the 5-PPG mark. Gee, also a professional baseball player, was familiar locally as a former member of the Syracuse Chiefs. Local favorite Bob Nugent filled in the offensive gaps with his crisp ball handling, averaging just over 3 points per game. Bill McCahan, Jack Dugger and Ken Exel rounded out the squad.

Despite poor attendance at the State Armory on Jefferson Street, Coach Bernhard "Bennie" Borgmann, one of the game's pioneer players, remained optimistic about his team. Borgmann had played for seventeen years, between 1919 and 1936, and is primarily associated with the Kingston Colonials and Original Celtics, both legendary teams. He packed an abundance of talent and knowledge into his five-foot-nine frame and demanded respect—and got it. Borgmann was tolerant with the Nationals, but patience and losing are hardly synonymous.

Born on November 22, 1900, in Haledon, New Jersey, Borgmann was nothing short of spectacular inside a gymnasium. As a member of Frank Morgenweck's Kingston, New York team, he had assisted in handing the Original Celtics' three losses in 1923, an astonishing feat during that era. But Borgmann was also an eyewitness to the death of both the Eastern and New York State Leagues. As a participant, he understood that the game was as dynamic as it was winsome.

In a twelve-team league, consisting primarily of small midwestern towns, the Nationals posted a 21-23 record in the Eastern Division, identical to that of the Toledo Jeeps. In the playoffs, the Nats would be beaten by Rochester, an upstate adversary, in four games. The Royals would be defeated 3 games to 1 by the Chicago American Gears.

For team management, much was copacetic. The season was a success despite a first-year financial loss; Central New Yorkers simply needed to embrace quality basketball, here in their own backyard, and that would take time. If the rivalries could be created, Biasone thought, the seats could be filled. Watching local cagers tackle—often physically—the Royals or Jeeps was worth a fair admission. He knew that. He just had to convince his audience; the team, however, was disappointed when the Buffalo Bisons, a team he had hoped to rival against, opted for a transfer to the Tri-Cities

The Jefferson-Clinton Hotel (foreground) is a mere point guard toss to the Jefferson Street Armory grounds (background).

Blackhawks (Moline and Rock Island, Illinois, and Davenport, Iowa). Overcoming a geographic identity complex remained a marketing challenge. Most Syracuse fans couldn't find Sheboygan on the map and thought that a Kautsky (Indianapolis) was a German frankfurter or a radical form of orthodox Marxism.

Without scouts, it was hard for professional team management not to keep at least one eye on the college ranks, especially after the war. The end of the 1945–46 college season is best remembered—as well it should be—for a giant of a man who would single-handedly change the sport. Standing at six foot ten and weighing 245 pounds, the thick-bespectacled figure of George Lawrence Mikan Jr. was intimidating, his talent extraordinary. Signing with Chicago, he played for them in only seven games at the end of the 1946 NBL season but scored an impressive 16.5 points per game!

During this era, professional basketball teams were as common as car dealers on East Genesee Street, or so it appeared. To settle the score of who was best, the *Chicago Tribune* sponsored an invitational tournament, the World

SYRACUSE NATIONALS

1946–47: THE PLAYERS

#45 JOHN CHANEY	FORWARD *
#40 JERRY RIZZO	FORWARD
#65 BOB NUGENT	GUARD *
#70 MIKE NOVAK	CENTER
#5 JOHN GEE	CENTER
#30 GEORGE NELMARK	GUARD
#75 JOHN MEEHAN	GUARD *
#25 STEVE SHARKEY	GUARD
#15 JACK DUGGER	GUARD

also
#25 BILL MCCAHAN *
    KEN EXEL *
COACH: BENNIE BORGMANN
UTILITY MAN : SYLVESTER LEONE
* Uniform numbers vary.

1946–47 SEASON	G	FG	FT	PTS
	44	888	570	2346

Co-owners Daniel Biasone and George Mingin bring a National Basketball League franchise to the city of Syracuse and into the State Armory on Jefferson Street. The Syracuse Professional Basketball Club is known as the "Nationals." The team colors are blue and gold. A preliminary game often begins at 7:30 p.m., with the main event at 9:00 p.m.

Professional Basketball Tournament (WPBT), to allow the best teams from various leagues to compete. In the WPBT, Mikan was elected Most Valuable Player after scoring one hundred points in five games and was also voted into the All-NBL Team, all while leading the Gears to the championship of the WPBT. It was an impressive entrance by the DePaul University graduate who was well on his way to basketball immortality—the Big Man Cometh!

THE 1947–48 SEASON: NO APPROBATION AT THE ARMORY!

Before the start of the season, Maurice White, the president of the American Gear Company and no stranger to entrepreneurism, felt like many of his predecessors: that he had the key to basketball's longevity. As owner of the American Gears of the NBL, he pulled the team out of the league. Management, including Biasone, was furious at the action. The egocentric White planned to create a twenty-four-team league called the Professional Basketball League of America (PBLA), in which he owned all the teams and arenas, but his "dribbles of grandeur" came to abrupt ending when the PBLA folded after just a month. The players of White's teams, including Mikan, were equally distributed among the eleven remaining NBL franchises.

Struggling during their second season, the Nats finished in fifth place with a 24-36 record. While the Mikan-led "Minneapolis tour de force" did much to draw attention to the league and the sport—particularly in the Midwest—progress was slow in coming east; it was not filling seats at the Armory, and the decline at the turnstiles was once again a disappointment.

During the fifty-game season, Syracuse faced Flint (6-0), Indianapolis (4-2), Oshkosh (3-3), Sheboygan (3-3), Toledo (3-3), Tri-Cities (2-4), Minneapolis (2-4), Anderson (1-5), Fort Wayne (0-6) and Rochester (0-6).

Newcomer Jim Homer, who averaged 12.3 PPG while totaling 698 points, was the team arsenal. Identical to the previous season, the ever aggressive Mike Novak averaged 9.1 PPG and finished second in individual scoring with 548 points. Jerry Rizzo, slightly shrouded by the shadow of Homer, increased his point production to 537 but fell to 8.9 PPG. John Chaney, Steve Sharkey and Bob Kitterman each managed to compile just under

SYRACUSE HARDWOOD LEGEND

Paul Norman Seymour

Position: Guard-Forward
Height: 6-1
Weight: 180 lbs.
Born: January 30, 1928, in Toledo, Ohio
High School: Woodward in Toledo, Ohio
College: University of Toledo
SYR Uniform #: 25 - 8 - 5

Began career with the Bullets the BAA during the 1947–48 season...played his final game with Syracuse during the 1959–60 season...scored over 1,000 points during the 1954–55 championship season...named to 1953-1954-1955 All-Star teams...a durable playmaker who always ranked high in assists per game...a fan favorite!

Paul began coaching at the age of twenty-nine with Syracuse in 1956–57...he was also a coach for St. Louis, Baltimore and Detroit...he finished first in Western Division with St. Louis, 1960–61—a team that included Bob Pettit, Cliff Hagen, Clyde Lovellette, Larry Foust and Lenny Wilkens...lost to Boston in finals...he was a fierce competitor.

CAREER NBA	G	FG	FT	PTS
	600	2012	1736	5760

300 points, while George Nelmark and newcomers Paul Seymour and John "Brooms" Abramovic rounded out the squad.

As a college freshman, a handsome six-foot-one guard had played at the University of Toledo (1945) and had exemplified tremendous hardwood skills, so much so that a year later he was no longer at school but rather playing for the Jeeps. Following a brief stint with New Orleans, he was signed by Baltimore of the BAA. Appearing in just twenty-two games, the youngster was then sold to Syracuse. His name was Paul Seymour. While the Nats were impressed with his potential, few would have expected that such a brilliant career was in store for the Ohio native.

Finishing twenty games behind Rochester in the East (fourth place), the Nats would make the playoffs—but, as anticipated, it was not a pretty sight. The team was swept, in three straight games, by the Anderson Duffey Packers.

After the PBLA had died, Mikan actually thought that he was a free agent, but such was not the case, nor was it an obstacle when "the First NBA Superstar" happily signed with Minneapolis. In addition to Mikan, the Lakers had Jim Pollard, the first player to genuinely play the game "above the rim." The lethal combination enabled the team to triumph in the Western Division with an impressive record of 43-17. Mikan would set a new single-season scoring record for the NBL (1,195), nearly doubling the existing record (632) set during the previous season by the Royals' Al Cervi. In an impressive display, the Lakers defeated the Royals, 3-1, to claim the championship.

The WPBT took place at Chicago Stadium in 1948, and eight teams had been invited. The Lakers, who defeated the Wilkes-Barre Barons and the Anderson Packers, advanced to the tournament championship against a black team from New York City, the New York Renaissance (or the Rens). In what would be the final WPBT, the Lakers beat Sweetwater Clifton and the Rens, 75–71.

THE 1948–49 SEASON: A SYRACUSE SHUFFLE

In the management's own words, "To darken an already dismal picture, Rochester, Minneapolis, Fort Wayne, and Indianapolis jumped the NBL in favor of the rival Basketball Association of America (BAA) after the 1947–48 race." A disconsolate Biasone continued to be implored to withdraw from professional basketball. While his business prowess agreed, his sentiment did not. With encouragement from his friend Ike Duffy, a businessman, future railroad magnate and then owner of the Anderson club, Danny Biasone persevered with a plan.

The Nationals' "recipe for success" began by recruiting Leo F. Ferris, then a talented team executive (Tri-Cities and would become the Nats' executive director), to reorganize the Syracuse team. The Elmira native began his basketball career when he and Ben Kerner founded a Buffalo franchise in the NBL. Ferris convinced Biasone that an infusion of cash was necessary, so team management approached a score or more of leading Syracusans and sold twenty-five shares of stock at $1,000 each. The first use of their new finances was an extensive publicity campaign, which preceded the aggressive and strategic pursuit of basketball talent. But both, if successful, would require increased seating capacity, which could be gained by transferring home games to the State Fair Coliseum, which the team also secured. In hindsight, the plan was as utopian as it was efficacious.

It was Honoré de Balzac who affirmed: "There is no such thing as a great talent without great willpower." Had the French novelist lived in Rochester and seen a Royals game during this period, he would have certainly been referring to a scrappy character by the name of Al Cervi. When salary

SYRACUSE HARDWOOD LEGEND

William A. Gabor

Position: Guard-Forward
Height: 5-11
Weight: 170 lbs.
Born: May 13, 1922
High School: Binghamton Central in Binghamton, NY
College: Syracuse University
SYR Uniform #: 35-7

Began career with Syracuse during the 1949–50 season…played his final game with the Nationals, during the 1954–55 season…scored over 600 points in three of six seasons with the Nats…named to 1953 All-Star team…Billy, or "Bullet Bill," was a solid playmaker who averaged 9.8 points per game…injuries forced his retirement…he was drafted by Rochester in 1948 BAA draft.

Bill averaged 12.1 points per game during his freshman year before joining the United States Army Air Corps in 1943…returned to the university in 1945 and played three more seasons, finishing with a (then) team record 1,344 career points…Syracuse retired his jersey on March 1, 2009.

CAREER NBA	G	FG	FT	PTS
	307	1080	837	2997

negotiations impaired his ability to stay in Rochester, Cervi turned to Syracuse as the new player-coach. Central New York fans were more than happy with the new addition; in fact they were ecstatic. They loved Cervi as a player and detested him as a foe. Cervi would head a team that now included Dolph Schayes, Johnny Macknowski, Ed Peterson, Jim Homer, Billy Gabor, Jerry Rizzo, Bob Calihan, Paul Seymour, Hank O'Keefe and John Chaney (players listed in PPG order).

Both Schayes and Cervi performed brilliantly, bolstering the team's PPG by 12.7 points (66.3) against a now ten-team league. Macknowski, Peterson, Homer and Gabor all averaged more than 6.0 PPG and filled the gaps nicely. During the 63-game season—3 more than the previous season—the Nationals had posted 4,179 total points, up from 3,216. Winning 40 of the 63 contests, the Cervi-led Nats finished second in the East, 8.5 games behind the division-winning Anderson Duffey Packers, and made the playoffs.

Leading the league in numerous categories, including total scoring points (872), average points per game (13.8) and foul shooting, was Tri-Cities

An unrelenting player-coach, Al Cervi (1917–2009) instilled the values of the game, especially winning, into his teammates.

colossus (six-foot-ten) center Don Otten. For the Nationals, Dolph Schayes at 12.8 PPG was good enough to place third among league leaders in scoring, while Al Cervi's 12.2 PPG put him eighth.

In the opening round of the NBL playoffs, the Nationals defeated the Hammond Calumet Buccaneers (2-0) but lost to Anderson during the Eastern Division Semifinals (3-1). The Anderson Duffey Packers would defeat the Oshkosh All-Stars (3-0) to take the league championship.

Honors and accolades showered the Nats, as a very deserving Al Cervi was named to the NBL's All-League team and voted Coach of the Year, and Schayes captured Rookie of the Year honors. More importantly, the move west to the Coliseum on the grounds of the New York State Fair bolstered attendance—the team's home opener drew 4,674 fans.

PART II
The Syracuse Nationals

Chapter 3
THE FRANCHISE'S
FIRST STAR, 1949–1954

S even months after U.S. president Harry S. Truman unveiled his "Fair Deal" program, six teams from the NBL (Anderson, Denver, Sheboygan, Syracuse, Tri-Cities and Waterloo), plus the Indianapolis Olympians—an expansion team scheduled to begin play in the NBL in 1949–50—joined the Basketball Association of America (BAA). It would be these seventeen teams, realigned to form three divisions, that would represent the National Basketball Association (NBA).

Despite the equitable mentality of the time, another new league drew skepticism—more concern about a great sport that couldn't seem to get beneath its problems. Such a phalanx of teams in an America defined by the railroad instead of the airplane meant that Denver may as well have been San Diego or some other far west team. League integration would be an immediate concern, and a paramount one at that. Since travel by rail was already indefatigable, the thought of coast-to-coast travel was incomprehensible, both to the players' well-being and the owners' pockets. Yet another consideration would be fan acceptance. When the Celtics played the Knicks, they traveled by train, passing through Massachusetts, Rhode Island and Connecticut—their fan base. But unlike the Red Sox, who traveled the same path, few people, if any, lined station observation decks in anticipation. Expansion had its detractors.

The BAA brought its own set of issues to the new league, including low-scoring games and poor attendance (the NBL had better players), along with confrontations (scheduling conflicts) because many teams shared arenas and even owners with hockey teams. It was not a pretty picture, but it was one that needed to be addressed quickly if the new league was going to succeed. Spoke an anonymous critic, "The BAA was as solid all right, as solid as ice!"

Serving as the first president of the NBA was the familiar face of Maurice Podoloff, a U.S. lawyer and basketball and ice hockey administrator. Discovering the perfect blend between "wood and water" would be his challenge—and one he welcomed. Although the 1949–50 season was the fourth rendition of the organization, it is recognized as the *first* official season of the NBA. As one of the premier orators of the time, Sir Winston Churchill so eloquently stated, "There is nothing wrong with change, if it is in the right direction."

A CENTRAL NEW YORK HERO: DOLPH SCHAYES

At six foot eight and 220 pounds, the Adonis figure of Adolph "Dolph" Schayes was as formidable as it was striking, both on and off the hardwood. Born on May 19, 1928, in New York City, he attended DeWitt Clinton High

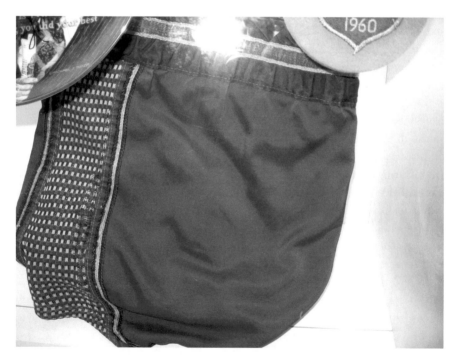

The pants worn by Syracuse Nationals star Dolph Schayes adorn a case inside the Naismith Memorial Basketball Hall of Fame.

School in the Bronx, New York, before playing his college basketball at New York University, 1944–48. As a sixteen-year-old freshman, Schayes exuded athleticism, with a proficiency so convincing that he made the NYU varsity squad. On the court, he was simply magnificent.

In 1948, one year before the NBA merger, both Syracuse of the NBL (who obtained rights from Tri-Cities) and the New York Knicks of the BAA were competing for the talented Dolph Schayes—understandably so, considering the demographics. But since the latter had controlled expenses by adopting a salary limit for first-year players, this left the Nationals the option of offering more money—the figure Schayes was hoping for. Already a popular fixture with New York fans, Schayes preferred to stay in the city, but Knicks owner Ned Irish refused to break the salary cap. Thus the talented twenty-year-old headed upstate, to his new home in Onondaga County.

A multifaceted player, whose durability was exemplary of his dedication, Schayes brought a new standard of performance to the Nationals; he would be the top scorer in thirteen of the club's seventeen-year existence. As his strength increased, so did his rebounding skills—another tool in an already impressive arsenal. His willingness to drive relentlessly through the lanes was as measured as it was instinctive. Combine this with a precision-crafted two-hand set shot and free throw perfection, and you have yourself the making of a legend. Schayes was beyond what every Nats fan was hoping for; he was an answer to their prayers. As this author has often overheard, "He was the best thing to happen to Syracuse since salt!"

THE 1949–50 SEASON: DIGGER'S DRAGOONS

In his role as vice-president of the Nats and member of the board of governors of the NBA, Biasone saw a competent Syracuse front office as a critical component to their success. Since verisimilitude requires detailed implementation, he assembled an enterprising team.

John C. Johnson is a well-known "iceman" around Syracuse, serving as vice-president of the Syracuse Hockey Club in 1930 and as president and operator of the club from 1936 to 1938. In 1948, he was elected president of the Syracuse Professional Basketball Club, with the goal of providing clean and wholesome basketball entertainment to the public. Assisting him was Art Deutsch, the new general manager of the Nats, having moved up from his promotional duties in 1948–49. Deutsch, who had worked for both the Buffalo Bisons and the Tri-Cities Blackhawks of the NBL, brought with him much-needed public relations experience. His assistant general manager was Syracuse native Ted Eckermann, the former assistant publicity director. Handling public address duties at the Coliseum, while assisting in play-by-play broadcasts and planning exhibition tours, was a large part of Eckermann's responsibilities.

Complementing the team were Vice-Presidents Albert C. Deisseroth and Harry Marley, along with Secretary-Treasurer Berard W. Sarno. The directors of the Syracuse Nationals included Howard Barth, Tony Bersani, Biasone, Albert C. Deisseroth, R. Edward Dorsey, Vic Hanson, John C. Johnson, Harry Marley, Edward Mosler and Dr. William Vickers.

The excitement generated by the Nats' season opener at the Coliseum on Thursday, November 3, felt fresh and invigorating despite the lackluster attendance (2,476). Compiling the first of four straight wins—the earliest two against the Denver Nuggets, the second of which was played in Auburn, New York—the Nationals appeared comfortable in their new league. Following a November 10 loss to the St. Louis Bombers, they began a twelve-game consecutive winning streak that would take them through the first week of December. (The streak even included a win against the Nuggets in Oneida, New York.) When the year 1949 concluded, the Nats were 24-4, having lost only to St. Louis, Rochester, Anderson and Washington. It was a superb display of basketball!

Memorable Games

Thursday, November 24, 1949, Syracuse, 125 v. Anderson, 123
Five Overtimes—122 Personal fouls—56 for Syracuse

Sunday, March 26, 1950, Syracuse, 91 v. New York, 83
OT in Eastern Division Finals—Third Straight Win!

Thursday, January 17, 1952, Minneapolis, 110 v. Syracuse, 105
Schayes Dominates! 41 Points, 23 Free Throws

Thursday, January 7, 1954, Fort Wayne, 79 v. Syracuse. 67
Smallest Crowd?—1,433 fans watch!

Tenacious in their victory pursuit, Cervi's dragoons dominated their combatants—the highlight of the second half being the eight-game winning streak that began on Thursday, February 2, against Indianapolis and ended with a loss to Denver on Tuesday, February 21. They were as zealous as they were adept—simply spectacular! The team finished the regular season 51-13, with momentum in their favor; it would prove to be the highest winning percentage and most wins in team history!

The Nationals captured the Eastern Division Semifinals (2-0) versus the Philadelphia Warriors and took the finals (2-1) versus the New York Knickerbockers. Although seemingly undeniable and predestined, ahead lay Minneapolis and Mikan.

Having won seven straight playoff games—downing Chicago, Fort Wayne and Anderson—the Lakers were tyrannizing and relentless. They too felt ordained. But player-coach Al Cervi, who seemed to bask in adversity, welcomed the challenge—if "Digger" was intimidated by anyone, it was rarely seen. It was his tenacity and defensive skills that would drive the club, and he knew it. While the rivalry between Syracuse and Minneapolis was bitter, it could not match the hatred already possessed by Rochester fans for the Lakers—Al Cervi was their favorite son, and they would have his back in Syracuse if required.

As the pendulum of momentum swung, during game one, the contest remained evenly matched. With one minute remaining, the Nats were up by a bucket, 66–64. The Lakers then called a play for Jim Pollard. Rookie Bud Grant (yes, that Bud Grant, the future Minnesota Vikings football coach) brought the ball up court and then passed it to his target, but Pollard was staunchly defended, so he returned the ball back to a stunned Grant. Confounded, Grant launched a "Hail Mary" to tie it up. The Central New York crowd just stood in disbelief.

Cervi then took things into his own hands; opting for a game-winning shot wasn't unusual behavior for "Digger," but successfully maneuvering around Mikan was. In a valiant move toward the basket, the shot was blocked by Mikan and retrieved by Grant, who quickly threw it to rookie Bob Harrison, who popped a forty-footer for the win; 68–66, Lakers. The Nats were devastated, nobody more so than Cervi.

"My friends and I were some of the last spectators to leave the Coliseum," spoke Jack Nelson. "It was just heartbreaking, a game I will never forget. I still have the orange ticket stub. Cost me $2.40 for the ticket, but it was worth every damn cent!"

The following day, Sunday, April 9, 1950, the Nats once again stood before the Lakers at home, determined to vindicate their loss. Looming over the court was not only George Mikan but also a smoke screen so thick that you could hardly see down court. The local press had leaked a story that the giant was allergic to smoke, so not a soul in the Coliseum could be seen without a cigar or cigarette. While it didn't stop Mikan, who netted thirty-two points, it did slow the Lakers, who lost 91–85. Match even, 1-1.

As the series shifted to Minneapolis on Friday, April 14, the Nats were hoping for at least a split; the Lakers, always formidable at home, thought only of a sweep. Although the game would not be held in the Minneapolis Aud, but instead inside the St. Paul Auditorium, the change in venue had no effect on the results; the Nats lost both, 91–77 and 77–69. The Syracuse strategy to pressure Pollard was thwarted by the efforts of both Mikan and Vern Mikkelsen. The series now stood 3-1, Lakers.

Back home, on Thursday, April 20, the Nats delivered an 83–76 victory in a must-win situation. The fans were just ecstatic, attributing everything to the win. "I went out and got myself a new suit at Learbury's, down on North Salina at Laurel, just for that game," spoke Michael DiRenzio. "Cost me $42.00; that's about a half a buck a point. Not bad." Still down 3-2, Syracuse remained optimistic, but this time they would play on the Lakers' home court, the Minneapolis Auditorium.

As game six ticked to a close, so did the dreams of the Nationals. Syracuse found themselves behind a 110–95 loss; Minneapolis had won the championship—the first team to win back-to-back crowns, beating Syracuse four games to two in the finals.

The Nationals management would later state that this was the year the team hit their zenith. In concurrence, most hoops historians view it as one of the most formidable Nats' offering in franchise history—mathematically a dominant statement despite not winning the championship.

Nats and Stats

As most are aware, statistical leaders exist for every NBA season and can provide a useful benchmark for comparison purposes. Those players who dominated during the year included: in points, George Mikan, Minneapolis (1,865); in assists, Dick McGuire, New York (386); in FG percentage, Alex Groza, Indianapolis (47.8); and in FT percentage, Max Zaslofsky, Chicago (84.3).

As for Syracuse, they could hold their heads high, especially during the playoffs, when Schayes, George Ratkovicz and Johnny Macknowski all averaged more than ten points per game, Alex Hannum delivered a .442 FG

SYRACUSE HARDWOOD HERO

George Ratkovicz

Position: Center-Forward
Height: 6-6
Weight: 220 lbs.
Born: November 13, 1922, in Chicago, Illinois
SYR Uniform #: 65 - 6 - 10

Began career when he was only nineteen years of age, playing thirteen games for the Chicago Bruins of the NBL, 1941–42…missed three seasons due to military service…also played for the Chicago, Rochester and Tri-Cities of the NBL…played three seasons for Syracuse…traded to Bullets in 1952 for Bill Calhoun…played his final game with Milwaukee during the 1954–55 season…was a charity stripe artist.

George averaged 8.6 PPG in his first league season and played in the finals, where the Nationals lost to the Lakers in six games…played 194 games for Syracuse…his 41.5 FG percentage was the sixth highest in the league during 1950–51 season…also ranked in the top ten in free throws (FT) and attempts (FTA).

CAREER NBA	G	FG	FT	PTS
	343	999	1143	3141

percentage and, despite the loss, Al Cervi lived up to expectations with more than fifty assists.

Finishing among regular season "League Leaders" were Dolph Schayes—in numerous offensive categories—and Al Cervi. Both performed brilliantly.

Court Comments

It was also a year of transformation, as Duquesne University's Charles Cooper became the first black man drafted by a league team, the Celtics, and a year of consistency, as Coach Nat Holman's City College of New York became the first (and last) college team to win both the National Collegiate Athletic Association (NCAA) and National Invitation Tournament (NIT) titles in the same year; they defeated Bradley in both championship games.

Speaking of transfiguration, since revenue-generating capabilities were often a function of arena capacity, imagine this contrast: Sheboygan, at a limit of 3,500, was the smallest venue and Syracuse established some middle ground at 7,500, while Chicago, at 21,000, was the largest facility. Intimacy, too, can have its limitations.

All-Time Team Winning Percentages

Rank	Year	Team	W-L	%
1	95–96	Chicago Bulls	72-10	.878
2	96–97	Chicago Bulls	69-13	.841
2	69–70	Los Angeles Lakers	69-13	.841
3	66–67	Philadelphia 76ers	68-13	.840
4	72–73	Boston Celtics	68-14	.829
5	46–47	Washington Capitols	49-11	.817
5	85–86	Boston Celtics	67-15	.817
5	91–92	Chicago Bulls	67-15	.817
5	06–07	Dallas Mavericks	67-15	.817
5	99–00	Los Angeles Lakers	67-15	.817
6	70–72	Milwaukee Bucks	66-16	.805
6	07–08	Boston Celtics	66-16	.805
6	08–09	Cleveland Cavaliers	66-16	.805
7	49–50	Syracuse Nationals	51-13	.797

In Boston, Red Auerbach was hired by team owner Walter A. Brown to replace Alvin "Doggie" Julian; the Celtics had slipped to a record of 22-46. A bad record in hand, however, meant a high draft pick in pocket, and the new coach felt immediately obligated to take a flashy local player—not the first guy to dribble behind his back, that was Bob Davies, but a player perhaps more proficient—a star hailing from Holy Cross. Bob Cousy was his name. The new coach—still a reflection of "old school" hardwood—lamented that a club didn't build a team with guards but rather built it around big men, so Auerbach didn't select Cousy. But the basketball gods, most likely from the North End of Boston, were yet to speak. Shortly after the draft, the Chicago franchise, which had selected Cousy, folded. This made him available for the dispersal draft, which is how he ended up in Boston. Fate had intervened, as Cousy's name was drawn from a hat; some claim that it was owned by Danny Biasone.

THE 1950–51 SEASON: A COLISEUM CONUNDRUM

A "more sensible structure" is how team management positioned it; less travel is how the players viewed it. This is in reference to the league's first contraction: six teams (Anderson Packers, Chicago Stags, Denver Nuggets, St. Louis Bombers, Sheboygan Red Skins and Waterloo Hawks) left the league, and by midterm, the Capitols had folded, bringing the number of teams in the organization down to ten.

An optimistic Nats team entered camp. Gone from the previous year's register were Ray Corey and Andrew Levane, while the Nats added to their roster second-round draft pick guard Gerry Calabrese from St. John's University, former Red Skins center Noble Jorgensen, first-round draft pick forward Don Lofgran from the University of San Francisco, former Capitols guard Fred Scolari and former Bombers guard Belus Smawley. Players who were drafted but did not play included Stan Christie, Paul Merchant, Paul Hickey, Mack Suprunowicz, Lou Arko, Bob Healey, Syracuse standout Bob Savage and Glenn Wilkes.

Witnessing the transition from college standout to pro player was always fascinating. For example, "meal-money"—often just a handful of dollars—was welcomed by the youngsters but considered "pocket change" to most vets. Near the Coliseum you could grab a bite at CerLo's

A pair of Nationals warm-ups donated to the Naismith Basketball Hall of Fame by Syracuse legend Paul Seymour.

SYRACUSE HARDWOOD HERO

Noble Gordon Jorgensen

Position: Center
Height: 6-9
Weight: 228 lbs.
Born: May 18, 1925
College: University of Iowa
SYR Uniform #: 13 - 6

Began career with the Pittsburgh Ironmen of the BAA, 1946–47...played his final game with Syracuse Nationals during the 1952–53 season...durable and accurate, "Jorgy" was a reassuring presence on the Syracuse hardwood...played 199 games in a Nats uniform...traded by the Blackhawks with cash to the Nationals for Ed Peterson (1950).

Jorgy gained tremendous respect during his 1949–50 season with the Red Skins—he finished third on the team in points (704)...one of five Nats players to score over 500 points during the 1951–52 season...he was traded by Syracuse to Milwaukee for Bob Lavoy on November 23, 1953.

CAREER NBA	G	FG	FT	PTS
	253	776	745	2997

just down the road at 1000 State Fair Boulevard or try whatever you could find open over on nearby Milton Avenue in Solvay. A little farther toward the city, you had the eateries on West Genesee Street, including the Grimlow Restaurant-Diner, if you weren't grabbing a bite at the Eastwood Sports Center, which was always an option over on James. Players could also try Mercurio's Restaurant at 2710 James Street or Mirbach's Restaurant over on Butternut—both reasonably priced. For a *special* occasion there was always downtown for dining and dancing. Andrews at 700 South Salina Street was a hot spot, as was Lorenzo's at 476 South Salina Street. Naturally, many more options were available; you could head north and hit Tino's Restaurant at 425 North Salina or drive even farther, out to Liverpool, for a Heids frankfurter. Syracuse can't beat Miami in the winter, but you can always find a good meal.

With productivity paramount, team strategy often capitalized on mismatches over plays, a fact understood by the six players who carried the bulk of that year's responsibility: Schayes (F-C), Scolari (G), Ratkovicz (C-F), Gabor (G-F), Jorgensen (C) and Hannum (F-C). All six played more than sixty games during a term that opened on Thursday, November 2, against the Pistons. The team won their first three games, but it was a roller coaster of a season—little momentum could be sustained. A loss here, two wins there, a couple more losses—the team wasn't playing as a cohesive unit. Scoring above the century mark six times, including during a season-high victory over the Indianapolis Olympians, 121–97, was good but not good enough. While Syracuse was outstanding at scoring (first of eleven), they were also adept at relinquishing the advantage (fourth of eleven).

The team's 32-34 record meant the playoffs, but it also meant fourth in the East. Finishing below the .500 level was an embarrassment coming off the previous year's crusade; it would also be the worst season-to-season decline in winning percentage in franchise history. In the semifinals versus Philadelphia, the Nats swept (2-0) but lost in the East Finals (3-2) to New York. Three Syracuse players scored more than 500 points during the season: Bill Gabor, George Ratkovicz and Dolph Schayes, the latter scoring 1,121 points.

The Royals won the championship, beating New York four games to three in the finals. It was a newly invigorated Rochester team, now months removed from their 75–73 loss during a six-overtime-periods marathon (January 6)—the league's longest game ever—that would not be repudiated.

The first annual All-Star Game, a showcase of the league's top players, was played in Boston, Massachusetts, on March 2, 1951. Participating for the Nationals was Dolph Schayes, while Red Rocha—a name that will become familiar—represented the Bullets. The East defeated the West 111–94, thanks to Ed Macauley of Boston, who received the first Most Valuable Player (MVP) award.

Nats Chats

Worth noting among statistical leaders for this season is the new category of rebounds, led by Dolph Schayes of the Syracuse Nationals at 1,080 (16.4 boards per game, 2.3 better than Mikan); he is the first leader recognized in the field and the only member of the Nationals to ever lead in this category.

While it was an exciting year, it was also a year for introspection. The game's detractors were rejuvenated on November 22, 1950, when Fort Wayne beat Minneapolis, 19–18, in the lowest-scoring game in history. Using stalling tactics—once a club got a lead, all they had to do was protect it—the pathetic display represented vulnerability in the league's luster. If integrity was a concern, a proactive response was needed.

THE 1951–52 SEASON: A NEW HOME

In an attempt to refine the game, the league widened the foul lane from six to twelve feet. "The Mikan Rule," as it appropriately became known as, limited a player's effectiveness close to the basket. Forever with a bull's-eye on his back, George Mikan had thwarted previous attempts to negate the Lakers' advantage, but this alteration seemed more personal. A team's offense now had to begin farther from the basket, opening up the lane for more defensive rebounding. "That should keep Mikan out of there and from executing his deadly 'drop step and hook shot,'" commented Nats coach Al Cervi. (The adjustment was expanded to sixteen feet in 1964.)

Speaking of regulations, the NBA adhered to the college playing rules with the following major exceptions: 1) all games are played in four twelve-minute periods; 2) each player is permitted six personal fouls; 3) substitutions are allowed at any time; 4) any player who is fouled and injured and cannot attempt his foul shot must be removed from the game for a substitute (and he can not reenter the game); 5) if a double foul occurs and participating players thereby incur a sixth personal foul, such players shall attempt the foul shot before leaving the game; 6) if a personal foul is called on a player in the last two minutes of the game, or in the last two minutes of an extra period, the player fouled cannot waive the foul shot but must attempt his try; if the attempt is missed, the ball remains in play, or if the attempt is made, play continues from out of bounds with opponent in possession; and 7) a zone defense will not be allowed.

The only major franchise change found the Tri-Cities Blackhawks relocating from the "Tri-Cities" area—Moline, Illinois; Rock Island, Illinois; and Davenport, Iowa—to Wisconsin to become the Milwaukee Hawks. The stability, which was refreshing to everyone, was particularly welcomed by the minor market ownerships such as Syracuse, which could now focus more energy on their team and less on their league.

Departing the Nats were Leroy Chollet, Alex Hannum (traded to Baltimore for Red Rocha), Don Lofgran (sold to Indianapolis), Johnny Macknowski, Ed Peterson (traded in December 1950 for Noble Jorgensen), Fred Scolari (traded to Baltimore for Red Rocha) and Belus Smawley (sold to Baltimore), while the Nats added to their roster rookie guard George King, rookie forward Wally Osterkorn, veteran center Red Rocha and second-round draft pick and LeMoyne College star Don Savage. Players who were drafted but would not play included Paul Horvath, Glen Anderson, Bob Wheeler, Roy Reardon, Tom Jackie and Ray Kirkwasser. John McConathy,

The Franchise's First Star, 1949–1954

SYRACUSE HARDWOOD LEGEND

Ephraim J. "Red" Rocha

Position: Center - Forward
Height: 6-9
Weight: 185 lbs.
Born: September 18, 1923, in Hilo, Hawaii
High School: Hilo in Hilo, Hawaii
College: Oregon State University
SYR Uniform #: 16

Began career with the St. Louis Bombers of the BAA during the 1947–48 season...played his final game with Fort Wayne during the 1956–57 season...scored over 800 points three times during his career…named to 1951 and 1952 All-Star teams...spent four seasons with Syracuse...durable, aggressive and an effective field goal shooter...later coached at University of Hawaii—"the Fabulous Five."

Red earned All-Pacific Coast Conference honors in 1945, 1946 and 1947 while playing center for Oregon State University...represented Baltimore in the first league All-Star Game in 1951...still shares, with former teammate Paul Seymour, the league record for most minutes in a playoff game with sixty-seven...sold by Syracuse to Fort Wayne.

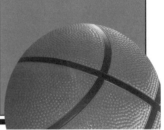

CAREER NBA	G	FG	FT	PTS
	480	1821	1501	5143

SYRACUSE HARDWOOD HERO

Walter Raymond Osterkorn

Position: Forward - Center
Height: 6-5
Weight: 215 lbs.
Born: July 6, 1928
High School: Amundsen in Chicago, Illinois
College: University of Illinois at Urbana-Champaign
SYR Uniform #: 17 - 8

Began pro career with the St. Paul Lights of the NPBL, 1950–51...spent four seasons with the Nats...played his final game with Syracuse during the 1954–55 season...durable and defensive, "Wally" or "Ox" was an imposing figure on the hardwood...scored a career-high 615 points during the 1953–54 season with Syracuse.

Wally had a brief stint with St. Paul before playing for Sheboygan in 1950... helped the Red Skins to a league-best 29-16 record...named to the NPBL's second team as a forward after averaging 13 PPG, sixth-best in the league...played over 200 games with Syracuse...posted 10.8 PPG during 1953–54 playoffs.

CAREER NBA	G	FG	FT	PTS
	204	453	530	1436

SYRACUSE HARDWOOD LEGEND

George Smith King Jr.

Position: Guard
Height: 6-0
Weight: 175 lbs.
Born: August 16, 1928 in Charleston, West Virginia
High School: Stonewall Jackson in Charleston, West Virginia
College: University of Charleston/Morris Harvey
SYR Uniform #: 3

Began career with Syracuse during the 1951–52 season...played his final game with Cincinnati during the 1957–58 season...was picked in the eighth round of the 1950 league draft by Chicago...an assist specialist...scored over 500 points in every season...later coached at West Virginia and Purdue...took latter to its only collegiate finals in 1969.

George was a durable playmaker and accurate shooter...a top-ten league leader in assists per game...he hit the series-clinching free throw and had a key steal in Nats' championship...sold by Syracuse to Royals in 1957...became the first American to give basketball coaching clinics in Africa...beloved Purdue coach and athletic director.

CAREER NBA	G	FG	FT	PTS
	411	1517	1185	4219

the Nats' first-round pick, landed with the Hawks, and Bato Govedarica wouldn't join the club until the 1953–54 season.

The Syracuse Nationals had a new home, the Onondaga County War Memorial. This multipurpose arena was conveniently located in downtown Syracuse, on State Street, and featured the first poured-in-place concrete roof in the United States. It smelled new, looked modern and created excitement within the community. But more importantly, at least to some of the players, it was a stone's throw from Salina Street, where much of the city's nightlife took place.

"It was a quick walk," a fan recalls. "One verse of 'Happy Trails' and you were on Salina Street. Looking north from the Chimes Building, you could see the Astor Theater, O'Shea's, Fleischman's, Howard and Loew's State Theater on the left side of the street and W.V. Haggerty on the right. At night it was our Broadway."

The War Memorial was an invigorating change from the cold confines of the fairgrounds. Although the Coliseum actually held more people, it was built in 1927 and lacked many modern amenities. Driving out to the fairgrounds, from James Street in Eastwood—less than ten miles away—felt like an eternity. Car heaters, a staple during the winter, didn't work all that well back then. Many players, gym bags in tow, would just jam themselves into available transportation and hope to generate maximum body heat. For fans, climate control depended on what you chose to wear to the game.

Memorial Hall, inside the War Memorial, was a very reflective place and a common destination for many of the early visitors to the building. Soldiers, sailors, marines, coast guardsmen, airmen and nurses would stand in silence reading the names of those inscribed on bronze tablets. Often a salute was given by a visitor in memory of a heroic and selfless sacrifice, a silent reminder of the cost of freedom.

In their new facility, the Nats welcomed 221,580 fans during basketball season. The team opened at home on Thursday, November 1, with a win against Fort Wayne, and by the end of the month they were 10-2 with a six-game winning streak under their belts. Handling the bulk of playing time were Rocha, Seymour, Schayes, King and Osterkorn.

The team battled through a four-game losing stretch in December and displaced the slide with nine consecutive January victories. Struggling a bit through February found them at 35-21 entering March. The second annual All-Star Game was played in Boston on Monday, February 11. The East, under the direction of Nats head coach Al Cervi, beat the West 108–91. Paul Arizin of Philadelphia received the game's MVP award.

A double-overtime victory over the Pistons, in Fort Wayne, 83–81, added a bit of momentum during the first week of March, and when the regular season closed on Sunday, March 16, the Nats were 40-26 and on top of their division.

The team won the Division Semis (2-1) versus Philadelphia but lost the Eastern Division Finals (3-1) versus New York. Superb defense and a balanced offensive attack—five players scored more than five hundred points—made anything less than a championship disappointing. Minneapolis, sporting an identical record, took the crown, beating New York four games to three in the finals.

Nats and Stats

While Al Cervi finished second in league charity stripe accuracy (.883), it would be from this point forward that Dolph Schayes would dominate the team's participation among "League Leaders." For the next nine seasons, Schayes would not score under 1,200 points.

Philadelphia's Andy Phillip, at 539, became the first player to break the 500-assist mark, and Rochester's Bobby Wanzer posted above the 90 percent mark from the free-throw line—two landmark achievements in the sport.

THE 1952–53 SEASON: OVERTIME AND ODIUM

Resolve, more applicable to the conflict in Korea at the time than to hardwood discord, was on the minds of many. Facing a tempting purchase offer from Ike Duffey (Anderson)—who was hoping to move the Nationals to Chicago—Syracuse management would not relent. While their lavish new surroundings were in stark contrast to the waning turnstile figures, management was resolute in their game plan.

Opulence wasn't just restricted to facilities, either, as Fred Zollner of the Pistons opted for the purchase of a DC-3 (1952), becoming the first owner to fly his players to away games. Both the mode of transportation and the transaction would have an enormous impact on the sport. From additional legroom to the ability to return home early enough to actually sleep in your own bed, the reduced travel time presented an entirely new realm of possibilities.

No longer a member of the Nationals this season were Gerry Calabrese, George Ratkovicz and Don Savage, while the Nats added to their roster Jim Brasco (drafted by the Nationals and later sold to the Hawks), Earl Lloyd (drafted by Syracuse from Washington in the dispersal draft) and Bob Lochmueller (drafted by the Nats). Players who were drafted but would not play included Bud Donnelly, Jim Kennedy, Harry Moore and Syracuse University standout Bob Roche. Ken McBride, from the University of Maryland, ended up playing for Milwaukee (1954–55). Picking up most of the minutes for the team would be Seymour (G-F), Schayes (F-C), King (G), Rocha (C-F) and Lloyd (F-C).

An optimistic Nationals team opened the season on the road against Philadelphia on Saturday, November 1, and lost a heartbreaker by a bucket, 84–86. But the Nats redeemed themselves the following night, at home, with a convincing 117–91 victory over the Warriors. Later that month, they put together a string of seven consecutive victories that helped them finish the year 18-11.

By January, the squad was really finding a comfort zone, as they managed a patch of nine consecutive wins; four victories topped the century mark, hitting an impressive 114 against New York on a Philadelphia neutral court. The All-Star Game, played in Fort Wayne on January 13, saw the West beat the East 79–75 and George Mikan of Minneapolis pick up a MVP award; Dolph Schayes and Paul Seymour represented the Nats. It was then give and take—a win then a loss—right up until the second week in March, when the team finished the season with five consecutive wins; this was consolation for the 47-24 record—second in the East and good enough for the playoffs. Mathematically, they were a solid team, scoring more points than they gave up. They were the third-best team in the league any way you cut it.

In their first playoff meeting, Syracuse confronted a new rival, Red Auerbach's Celtics. Not much better on paper, but very difficult to contain on offense, Boston scored more points than any other club in the league. Three members of the team scored more than one thousand points during the regular season: guard Bob Cousy, center/forward Ed Macauley and guard Bill Sharman. After the Nats dropped the first playoff game at home, 87–81, it was do or die.

Auerbach hated playing in Syracuse, detested the fans (he could describe certain individuals to you in detail) and despised the city—too cold! Spending a New Year's Eve in Syracuse was even a threat he held over his team, which they actually did once in penance for a loss. Auerbach was a constant target of taunting by Syracuse fans. "We would just ride his ass relentlessly," spoke an anonymous fan. "If his mother really didn't wear army boots, nobody in Syracuse believed it."

Back in the Boston Garden, Auerbach thought, "Now it's our turn." The Garden spared no fan from obstructed views, the smell of stale beer or a warm Boston welcome—Nats fans, check for your wallet. Quadruple overtime—that is what it took to decide this March 21 game, the game to end all games that didn't end. Not just any tussle, mind you, but the second and deciding contest in the first round of the playoffs. The odious encounter, embellished by 106 personal fouls, was so revolting that not only were players fighting players, but they were fighting the police as well. When it was concluded—as if games like this ever really are—a dozen players had fouled out, two had been ejected and the hometown referee had to be escorted out of the building.

Yeah, the two teams hated each other, but everyone hated Boston—it was like hating the Yankees—acceptable when not in vogue. Both teams were battling for the right to meet the Eastern champion Knickerbockers. The real rivalry, although some have claimed differently, centered on Boston's "smooth as silk" Bob Cousy and Syracuse's "tough as nails" Paul Seymour—two peas in an extremely competitive pod called the Eastern Division.

Auerbach, true to form, went to the partisan press early with his warning about Syracuse: "They play dirty…," blah, blah, blah. Syracuse player Paul Seymour reacted perfectly to Auerbach's allegations: "Do unto others…"

Syracuse broke out quickly, to an 8–0 lead, but Boston held their ground. Seymour was on Cousy like fly paper, while Auerbach was on both officials—Arnie Heft and Charley Eckman (a soon-to-be familiar name)—and the 11,058 fans were on the edge of their seats. By the time Cousy tossed in a thirty-footer to put an end to the first quarter, there had been more jabs than a Basilio-DeMarco ring battle. Stage now set: Nats up 22–21.

Auerbach, having seen enough, inserted Michigan State hatchet man Bob Brannum. "The Tank," a befitting moniker, averaged about 263 personal fouls per season, and he now positioned his assassin's sight directly at Schayes. When they started throwing punches, the Boston police charged the court. Parries were answered with personals, from multiple directions. Although the altercation ceased with the ejection of both players, it had intensified the playing atmosphere. When the game continued, so did the fouling.

Syracuse remained up at the half, 42–40, but fell down by three points at the end of the third quarter, 62–59. Seymour, who had hurt his ankle, was now in no shape to contain Cousy—and somebody needed to. There was little choice but to leave a pained Seymour backcourt and go four on five offensively. Syracuse pounded back and was up 77–76 when the buzzer sounded. But someone had fouled Cousy—the game wasn't over. When he converted the free throw, it was overtime.

Now what? Five Syracuse players had fouled out, while the rest were at or near the limit; one player had even been ejected (Schayes). The only reason Syracuse could floor five players was because the rules allowed for no fewer. Every player seemed to be operating on reserve power. With Seymour out of the picture, Cousy, Auerbach thought, would be the answer—certainly he could inflict more damage. Plus, if any player at the limit fouled him, it was an automatic two-shot technical. Both teams scored nine points during the first extended segment.

By the end of the second overtime, the score remained deadlocked, 90–90. The "Boys from Boston" also had foul trouble—down to five men, four at the limit. Despite fatigue and injury, Syracuse wouldn't give an inch. With just under twenty seconds remaining in the third OT, and Syracuse up by a bucket, Cousy—who else but "the Houdini of the Hardwood"—got fouled. Sinking both, the game was tied, 97–97. Syracuse drove down and dropped a bucket, 99–97, before the Green Team called time-out. Although everyone in the Garden knew that Cousy would get the ball, nobody could stop him; when the more than twenty-foot push shot went through the hoop, it was 99–all.

During the fourth overtime, Boston's Chuck Cooper picked up his sixth personal, which now allowed Syracuse two free throws every time he committed a non-shooting foul. The incident seemed to revitalize the Nats, who rang up five unanswered points, 104–99, advantage Syracuse. With three and a half minutes remaining, Cousy took over; he drew a foul and then made the shot. Celtics, down four, tapped in a missed shot; now down two, they intercepted a pass for an easy layup—score tied, 104–104. Two more Syracuse fouls, with made free throws, then turned the momentum in favor of the Celts. At the end of the fourth addition, there would be no more: 111–105, Boston.

It was a game of records, a pastime of pain, a reflection of character and a diversion of disdain. The winning team shot only 41 percent from the floor but sank thirty-seven straight shots from the charity stripe. The player who scored the most points, Cousy at fifty, only scored seven points in the first half; his thirty-for-thirty-two performance from the line still stands as a legendary achievement—at one point during overtime, Cousy sank eighteen straight.

On the dark side, twelve men had fouled out—seven for Syracuse, five for Boston—during the 106-personal-foul marathon, a record that stood until 1994. Free throw attempts (128) and free throws made (108) were as common as a Massachusetts liberal attitude. Speaking of liberal, how about those refs? As one Syracuse fan put it, "I thought I was watching the movie *Snow White*; you know: whistle while you work!"

Syracuse zealots—always willing to forgive but never willing to forget—also recalled the event the next time Boston played in Syracuse. Five thousand cardboard hatchets with Mr. Brannum's name on them were tossed by spectators onto the hardwood floor.

Vindication for the Nats came in the form of three Celtics losses to the Knickerbockers in the semis; it was anticlimactic but enjoyable. It was the first time Boston had ever made it past the opening round; unfortunately for Nats fans, it was not their last.

The season ended with Minneapolis winning the championship, beating New York four games to one in the finals.

Numbers and Notes

A stellar Dolph Schayes dominated the "League Leaders" board, picking up placements in points, charity tosses and grabs. Both George King and Paul Seymour also left solid assist marks among top performers.

The year saw the emergence of Philadelphia's Neil Johnston, who led the league in points (1,564) and FG percentage (45.2). Johnston would lead the league in scoring for three consecutive seasons: 1952–53, 1953–54 and

1954–55. This would also mark the first year, of eight, that Boston guard Bob Cousy would dominate the assists category.

Rookie of the Year honors went to Don Meineke of Fort Wayne; he would later become familiar to Upstate New York fans as a member of the Royals.

THE 1953–54 SEASON: THE "BANDAGED BRIGADE"

Still in its infancy, the medium of television was attracting considerable attention; it excited visionaries who saw it as a way to transform many actions including sports. Landing a contract with the DuMont Television Network to broadcast thirteen games was a feather in the league's cap, exciting both players and team management. The company, known perhaps best today for the classic thirty-nine *Honeymooners* episodes (1955–56), was excited about the game of basketball and what it had to offer viewers. Although the network had a promising beginning, prohibitive costs, regulations and partnerships would eventually lead to its demise; DuMont ceased broadcasting in 1956, just days from celebrating its ten-year anniversary and before having a chance to realize its hardwood dreams.

While the media attention was a tremendous boost for the sport, instability in any form, such as Indianapolis folding prior to the start of the season, was not. Each time another franchise fell, Syracuse team management would cringe; was attrition an isolated case or a trend? If it was the latter, certainly the Nats did want to be a part of it. Once again the city would come close to losing its franchise; this time the suitor was Detroit, but a rallying group of 150 enthusiasts thwarted the effort with a $200,000 stock sale purchase of the team. Central New York Basketball, Inc. (CNYB) was formed and Danny Biasone unanimously elected as president of the corporation.

It would be a season recalled for many reasons—some envisioned, others not. After appearing in only 38 games last season, Al Cervi decided to step off the hardwood and concentrate full time on coaching. For a man whose effervescence was unmatched, it was a sentimental departure. Cervi was a player who thrived on competition and loved all 202 games of it in a Nats uniform. With his trademark fortitude in tow, he left the floor as one of the greatest defensive players in history.

Riddled with injuries—every coach's nightmare—the "Bandaged Brigade," as the Nats were being affectionately called, just couldn't overcome their misfortune. From Seymour's broken thumb to a pair of broken hands (Lloyd and Schayes), convalescence was as common as a winter cold. If

SYRACUSE HARDWOOD HERO

William McGill Kenville

Position: Guard - Forward
Height: 6-2
Weight: 187 lbs.
Born: December 1, 1930, in Elmhurst, New York
College: St. Bonaventure University
SYR Uniform #: 15

Began career with Syracuse, 1953–54...they called him "The Rookie"...played his final game with Detroit during the 1959–60 season...tough and accurate, "Billy" was excellent from the charity stripe...selected by Syracuse in the 1953 league draft...durable and dependable...played three seasons with Nats...logged over 6,700 league minutes.

Billy was sold by the Nationals to Fort Wayne on October 3, 1956... averaged 7.1 PPG during 1954–55 championship season with the Nats...scored 582 points, a career season high, with Fort Worth (1956–57)...played with Alex Hannum, Red Rocha and George Yardley at Fort Wayne...a fan favorite.

CAREER NBA	G	FG	FT	PTS
	345	848	738	2434

anything positive came from it, it was Schayes's claim that his shooting improved—a scary thought for any competitor having to deal with this charity stripe master—as he would nurture and develop his opposite hand.

Jim Brasco, Noble Jorgensen, Bob Lochmueller and Red Rocha departed the Salt City, while the Nats added to their roster Ed Earle, Bato Govedarica, Bill Kenville (drafted by the Nationals), Dick Knostman (drafted by the Nationals), Bob Lavoy (traded by Milwaukee to Syracuse for Noble Jorgensen), Royals guard Al Masino, Jim Neal (drafted by the Nationals) and Warriors center Mike Novak—a five-game sentimental addition. Players who were drafted but would not play included Al Bailey, Garrett Beshear, Glen Dille, Joe Hughes, Bill Hull, LeMoyne College star Bill Jenkins, Andy McGowan, Gerald Nappy and Warren Shackelford.

A ritual among many players was washing out their uniforms at night. Hotel and apartment sinks were often filled with team colors, with rusty battle scars left by heating radiators where the uniforms were often left to dry. Repairs might also be done by a player's wife or taken to the Joe Charles Sport Shop over in Fairmount Fair Shopping Center, which handled some alterations. The team's attractive warm-ups were made by Coane, located in Philadelphia. While fans loved the red satin button-up knit jackets they had, with the three-color piping (black, yellow and orange) and "SYRACUSE, NATS" on the back, they were overburdened to remember just when that was—Nats identity alterations were common.

Halloween night saw the Nationals lose the season opener in Philadelphia to the Warriors, 73–79. Avenging the loss at home the following evening in front of a record crowd (7,859), the team finished the mediocre month of November 9-8, just above the .500 mark. December would begin cold, including a four-game losing streak, but improve with both a three- and four-game victory march.

Dolph Schayes and Paul Seymour represented Syracuse in the All-Star Game played in New York City on January 24, with the East beating the West 98–93 in overtime. Bob Cousy won the game's MVP award. Those lucky enough to witness the game caught Marty Glickman behind the microphone with Lindsey Nelson. A graduate of Syracuse University, Glickman was a familiar face and also a former all-American football player.

A decisive road win, over Fort Wayne, ignited a seven-game winning streak for Syracuse that took them into the middle of January. The team waffled a bit but finished the month 29-19. February proved to be a typical Nats month, back and forth with little momentum, but as spring began to break, the team took six of eight games in March to finish the season at 42-30, tied with Boston.

With a tiebreaker now in order, the Nationals dueled with Boston on Wednesday, March 17, at the Garden. An impassioned Syracuse team elbowed their way to a suspense-filled overtime victory, 96–95. It simply could not have happened at a better time. With playoff mentality intact, the Nats then defeated the Knickerbockers (2-0) for the right to challenge Boston in the Eastern Division Finals. (The league was experimenting with a round-robin tournament for the first round.)

Three straight playoff victories over the "Shamrock Squad," two at home and one in Boston, made it clear that Syracuse would be a force to contend with. Now it was off to Minneapolis for a tough series against the Lakers in the finals.

The transition game favored Minneapolis; a rebound from Mikan meant an outlet pass up court, likely to Martin or Pollard, with the other in place for an uncontested layup. When the league widened the lane in 1951, the game picked up pace, and teams like the Lakers followed, albeit reluctantly from a certain plodding big man.

It was preconceived by the Lakers that they would be facing the Knickerbockers in the finals, not Syracuse, the team they had defeated for their first league title in 1950. When the "Bandaged Brigade" hit the hardwood in game one, the Lakers saw three players in casts and everyone else in disbelief. The local newspaper, the *Syracuse Herald Journal*, even ran a photograph of the team poised as a "fife and drum" corps, with Coach Al Cervi leading his injured brigade (March 3, 1954). But the Nats split in Minneapolis and then took one out of three home.

Now down 2-3, the Nationals headed back to Minneapolis for the weekend, beginning Sunday, April 11. A miracle shot, with three seconds remaining, gave the Nats a 65–63 win. Jim Neal, one of the few not wearing a cast, caught an unexpected pass from Paul Seymour and just unloaded a thirty-footer. But the miracle carried no further, as the team found themselves behind an 87–80 loss in game seven. The Lakers were now the first team to win three consecutive NBA Championships. For the Nationals, it had been an incredible run, an exhilarating display of athletic prowess and the quintessence of courage. To say that the Syracuse fans were proud of their team would be an understatement.

Numbers and Notes

Among league front-runners was the Nationals' Dolph Schayes in the usual categories; playmaker Paul Seymour garnered accolades in charity tosses and assists, and Earl Lloyd led in personal fouls (303), this in the face of a new rule—two fouls per quarter. As for the latter, on October 31, 1950, Lloyd became the first African American to play in a league game, against Rochester. It is hard enough to play in this league with the criticism, but to endure the constant harassment this man was exposed to is incomprehensible.

As for the game's evolution, on February 13, 1954, future Nationals player Frank Selvy, then of Furman University, scored one hundred points in a game against Newberry College—a positive sign for a sport that had been criticized for being lackluster at times.

The street signs at the corner of James Street and North Midler Avenue, just a half-court pass from the Eastwood Sports Center. *Photo by author.*

Chapter 4

A GUT-WRENCHING CHAMPIONSHIP, 1954–1955

Finishing second satisfies few coaches, and Al Cervi wasn't one of them. At 42-30, and despite the injuries, the team was far better than the record indicated—they out-pointed their opponents, played better and, in a Pythagorean analysis of their wins v. losses, outshined the league. Their loss in the finals (4-3) to John Kundla's Minneapolis phalanx was heartbreaking. Matching the top three players, on both teams, in season point production favored Syracuse—albeit by an ever-so-thin layer, less than a bucket per game—but was *not* good enough for a championship. This fact, among others, irritated the hell out of a fierce competitor like Al Cervi.

When the Nats arrived in camp at the end of the summer, they were confident and upbeat. Their marquee names—Schayes, Seymour and Rocha—still instilled fear among opponents, and the team looked promising. The Nats added three rookie cagers to their scorecard: center Red Kerr out of University of Illinois at Urbana–Champaign; a six-foot-four guard from Indiana University, Dick Farley; and Duquesne University forward Jim Tucker. Departing the roster were Ed Earle, Bato Govedarica, Dick Knostman, Bob Lavoy, Al Masino, Jim Neal and Mike Novak. The Nats also acquired Connie Simmons from Baltimore in the dispersal draft on November 28.

Before the season had even begun the basketball gods intervened with two major events. On September 24, 1954, just days before the first tipoff, George "Mr. Basketball" Mikan, at the age of twenty-nine, retired from the game. Then—as if that alone was not enough to ignite Nationals fans—on

SYRACUSE HARDWOOD LEGEND

John G. "Red" Kerr

Position: Center - Forward
Height: 6-9
Weight: 230 lbs.
Born: August 17, 1932, in Chicago, Illinois
High School: Tilden in Chicago, Illinois
College: University of Illinois at Urbana–Champaign
SYR Uniform #: 10

Began career with Syracuse during the 1954–55 season...durable and fierce competitor...talented shot blocker...played his final game with Baltimore during the 1965–66 season...scored over 1,000 points in seven consecutive season...named to 1956-1959-1963 All-Star teams...a prolific rebounder—over 10,000 career grabs...beloved voice of the Bulls.

Red held the league record for most consecutive games played (844) until 1983...while coaching for Chicago, who went 33-48 in 1966–67, the Bulls became the first expansion team to win a playoff berth in its inaugural season...recipient of the Basketball Hall of Fame's John W. Bunn Lifetime Achievement Award.

CAREER NBA	G	FG	FT	PTS
	905	4909	2662	12,480

SYRACUSE HARDWOOD HERO

Richard L. Farley

Position: Guard - Forward
Height: 6-4
Weight: 190 lbs.
Born: April 13, 1932
College: Indiana University
High School: Winslow in Winslow, Indiana
SYR Uniform #: 14 - 12

Began career with the Nationals, 1954–55...played his final game with the Pistons during the 1958–59 season...tough and accurate, "Dick" was second to only Red Kerr in FG percentage during the Nats' 1954–55 championship season... played two seasons with the Nats...selected by Syracuse in the 1954 league draft...logged over 3,800 league minutes during three seasons.

Dick was traded by the Nationals, along with Earl Lloyd, to the Pistons for cash on June 10, 1958...played for the 1953 Indiana University national championship team...his career interrupted by service in the U.S. Air Force...a bridge, spanning the Patoka River, on State Road 61, was named in his honor.

CAREER NBA	G	FG	FT	PTS
	211	481	416	1378

October 30, the league adopted the 24-second shot clock. Two paramount proceedings, both advantage Syracuse!

Shrouded by these major announcements—as personal milestones can sometimes be in a team sport like basketball—is an accomplishment in consistency and durability. A six-foot-nine, 230-pound member of the Syracuse squad walked onto a basketball court, during every given opportunity, and it would not be until November 4, 1965, that people would realize that John G. Kerr had played in the last of 844 consecutive games.

Halloween night officially christened the season for Syracuse at home. (There was a game stricken from the record books on October 30 against Baltimore.) Across the court was the perfect haunting—the champion Lakers. Now led by veteran guard Slater Martin and forward Vern Mikkelsen, they were enhanced by center Clyde Lovellette, a year removed from the University of Kansas. The team had every intention of contending in the West, despite the loss—a big one at that—of Mikan. The Lakers took the meeting by three points, 97–94, at the War Memorial Auditorium. Martin, to this day, believes that if a healthy Mikan had played, the outcome of this season would have been far different—hypotheticals are indeed the fruit of contrarians. But if the big man's departure ignited anyone, it was Nats guard Paul Seymour—no. 4 sank nine field goals and netted seven free throws in a twenty-five-point statement.

NOVEMBER 1954

After a six-day break, the Nats headed to Boston on Saturday, November 6, to face their rivals in the Garden. Auerbach's artillery was fully equipped, and it showed; they trounced Syracuse, 107–84. Cousy, and fellow guard Bill Sharman, continued to find cracks water couldn't locate. Both proficient playmakers were enhanced by their adept six-foot-eight center, Ed Macauley. With little time to bask in self-pity, the Nats returned home immediately (Sunday, November 7) to tackle Milwaukee.

Lacking the depth of their previous two competitors, the Nats beat the Hawks convincingly, 97–80. Despite the efforts of rookie Bob Pettit, Milwaukee couldn't muster a convincing offensive attack—they looked loathsome. For Coach Cervi, it took three games, but the first win of the season was now under his belt; he could now focus on four straight road games, beginning with Fort Wayne on Thursday, November 11.

Everyone knew that the Pistons were tough at home, to put it mildly, and Coach Charles Eckman had his team primed for a challenge. Center

Larry Foust, at six foot nine, led the offensive threat, complemented by the accurate shooting of forward George Yardley, a year removed from Stanford. The Nats picked up the road game victory by a bucket, 88–86. Schayes, who had poured in twenty-two points against Boston five days ago, repeated his performance.

But the victory fire didn't burn long, as Syracuse dropped two in a row: the first to the Hawks, 85–72, on Saturday, November 13, followed by the Lakers, 99–92. The final game of the road trip was scheduled for Tuesday, November 16, in New York City against Philadelphia. The Warriors' one-two punch was forward Paul Arizin and center Neil Johnston. The Nats would squeak by in a one-point victory, 86–85. Now blessed by good luck, seven consecutive wins would follow.

The Nationals were bonding nicely, a tribute to everyone, especially their coach. "The loyalty on the team was unbelievable," recalls Bill Kenville. "They all took me under their wing, nicknamed me 'Rookie' and I never felt alone during my years with them." Making the move from the college ranks to a professional can be a difficult transition, complicated by a number of factors; guard Bill Kenville had one year under his belt during a season he would never forget. "I married shortly after graduation from St. Bonaventure University and immediately relocated with my wife to Syracuse," Kenville recalls. "In the summer I was invited by several of the Nats to join them at workouts."

A nine-point win at home over the Fort Wayne Pistons took place on Thursday, November 18. The Nats then looked west and headed for their first battle of the year against their now "Thruway" adversary, the Royals. Inside the Edgerton Park Arena, the Royals' well-balanced attack was led by veteran guard Bobby Wanzer. More of a chef than a server, Wanzer worked in tandem with his former Seton Hall teammate, guard Bob Davies. Together they fed forward Jack Coleman or center Arnie Risen. Edging out a single-point victory, the Nats took this game. Check please!

Returning home to face Boston, who had humiliated them earlier in the season, was in order on Sunday, November 21. An ignited offense, characteristic of this rivalry, led the Nationals to a 110–104 vindication. This was followed by a six-point victory over the Hawks on Thursday, November 25, before the Nats would play back-to-back games, away and then home, against New York.

Competing against the Knickerbockers in Madison Square Garden was always a thrill. Guard Carl Braun led their impartial attack, followed by forward Harry Gallatin, guard Jim Baechtold, forward Nathaniel Clifton and center Ray Felix. Attendance mushroomed when the Nats were in town, driven by the appearance of former NYU attraction Dolph Schayes. "Dolph was probably the toughest player for me to guard," spoke Gallatin, "a great outside shooter who could drive if you played tight on him." Syracuse took the first game against the Knicks 80–74 on Saturday, November 27, and duplicated the feat the following night, this time at home, 79–77. The latter would cap off the seven-game winning streak—their first notable run of the season—and bring the team to 9-4.

DECEMBER 1954

It was off to Philadelphia, a neutral court, to take on the Knickerbockers again on December 1. Grabbing the game, 88–86, New York handed the Nats their fifth loss of the season. Dick Farley scored sixteen points, while Connie Simmons dropped in a season-high twenty-three points. Back home the following night to battle Rochester, Syracuse once again triumphed, 82–78, to pick up their tenth win; Schayes tallied twenty-four points.

Facing the Nats next was Philadelphia in a three-game set, all at different venues: Philadelphia, Syracuse and New Haven, Connecticut. On Saturday, December 4, the Nats lost in Philly, 79–73, and then beat them the following night in Syracuse, 89–72. On neutral ground, the Nationals grabbed the final game on Tuesday, December 7, 88–81; Seymour popped ten field goals on his way to twenty-five points, tying his season high, and Billy Kenville sank twelve points, his fourth straight night in double figures.

On Wednesday, December 8, it was back to Rochester, where the Nats looked sluggish in a 105–78 beating. Only Johnny Kerr shined, as he sank ten field goals in a twenty-point effort.

Back home, on Thursday, December 9, was uplifting, as the team needed little prompting for back-to-back games against Boston, with a day off sandwiched between. Turning in a stellar performance, the Nats triumphed 120–107—a season-high point total. It took forty-two field goals and thirty-six free throws to do the damage in a very physical contest. Billy Kenville and Earl Lloyd impressed at twenty points apiece, and Red Rocha poured in twenty-one. Auerbach's posse prevailed in Boston, however, on Saturday, December 11, inching out a 94–90 victory—as usual, the rats were hungry, the Garden damp and the fans unruly.

In a physical but unprolific display, the team lost 96–87 to Philly at home on Sunday. Schayes turned in a fine performance, sinking ten field goals and a dozen free throws on his way to thirty-two points, but it wasn't enough.

Syracuse then began a long road stretch, one that found the team home only twice before the end of the year; they faced the Knickerbockers four times (once at home), the Lakers twice (once at home) and both the Royals and the Warriors out of town. The Nats split the first two games with New York, the second game being held in Boston. The team then had a couple of days to head to the Midwest before losing a close game to the Lakers, 86–83. On Sunday, December 19, they were back in Central New York hosting that same Lakers team, this time to a 108–93 victory.

"They were a good team that season—very aggressive with outstanding fan support," remembers the Knickerbockers' Harry Gallatin. "We knew we were in for a test from their defense. They were always tough…they tried to intimidate you to gain an advantage."

Five days off was welcomed by the players as time to visit family and do a bit of holiday shopping. The Nationals returned to the Garden to face off against New York on Christmas Day; in a heated contest, the team lost 109–101. Redemption came the following night, at home, 97–92. Syracuse then defeated the Royals on Tuesday in New York City, 84–82, before heading to Philadelphia the following night and dropping their final game of 1954, 72–70, against the Warriors.

Despite a record that now stood at 17-13, there was no blissful insouciance displayed by Al Cervi. He was uneasy and, perhaps more disturbing, unconvinced. His team lacked momentum; they could not put more than two victories together, and they needed to in order to win a playoff spot. They also needed to perpetuate a level of intensity—like the ferocity they always seemed to find against Boston, a team they loathed. To do that, Cervi believed, from this point forward it was time for his veteran players to "step up" and take control. That, he thought, would motivate the others.

The youngsters, after all, had displayed promise; rookie Dick Farley posted a season-high nineteen points against the Warriors (December 19), and Billy Kenville scored in double figures in all but six games, including twenty points against Boston (December 9). If the veterans could take charge, as Earl Lloyd did when he tallied twenty points against that same Boston team (also December 9) or as Red Rocha did when he sank twenty-two points against New York (December 26), that would inspire. Johnny Kerr could lead; he popped twenty points against Rochester (December 8), and of course there was the irreplaceable Schayes, who scored more than thirty points twice during the month! As for Paul Seymour, well, you could always "see more" from a player who could draw from his reserves almost at will, as he did dropping ten field goals against Philadelphia (December 7) and sinking a dozen against the Lakers (December 19). A healthy George King could also do some damage, something the team could look forward to down the stretch. The pieces were there; making them fit would be another story.

"I believe they really had a well-balanced team," recalls Boston guard Bill Sharman. "Everyone had a personal job to do…either on offense or defense…due to Al Cervi's leadership, they were a tough and physical team."

January 1955

The perfect way to begin any year, particularly if you are a Syracuse fan, is a victory over Boston. On this New Year's Day, at home, perfection was had in a stunning 108–102 victory. It would, however, be a prelude to mediocrity, as the Nats traded eight wins for eight losses during the month.

Given the 19-17 first-half accounting, Coach Cervi had to be particularly circumspect as the team entered the final stretch. No draconian measures needed; simply wisdom. As a hardwood cognoscente, he knew that his conduct not only reflected his own desires but also that of team management; an optimistic Biasone concurred.

Emerging on Thursday, January 13, during a game against Fort Wayne was a team whose desire was noticeably uplifted. A four-game winning streak followed, the longest since November, and included a 92–87 victory over their nemesis, Boston.

"Red [Auerbach] always wanted us to fast break as much as possible against the Nats," recalls Boston guard Bill Sharman. "He felt it would make us play and score better against their aggressive team."

The day after the Shamrocks victory, Friday, January 21, was "fight night" at the War Memorial. Local welterweight contender Carmen Basilio would tackle the tough German Peter Muller (also spelled Mueller). Many of the Nats had seen the charismatic Muller walking around town, either over at the Hotel Syracuse or along Salina Street, and became reasonably intrigued by him. But this was Central New York and Basilio country—the former onion farmer turned boxer hailed from the small hamlet of Canastota, not far from Syracuse. Carmen, a former marine, had little patience for his opponent, whom he beat in a unanimous ten-round decision. A Basilio fight such as this would outdraw an average Nationals game by a factor of two to one, a testament to where both sports stood in popularity at the time.

FEBRUARY 1955

With all cylinders firing, the Pistons defeated the Nats handily, 104–85, on Thursday, February 3, in Fort Wayne. After fifty games, Eckman's team stood 32-18 and was a clear threat to every team in the league. Such a loss made the Nats' trip to the Boston Garden the following night that much more difficult. There, Boston took command and handed Syracuse their fourth loss in a row, 114–88, but not before Red Rocha could sink twenty-one points. Billy Kenville, who had scored eighteen the previous night, powered his way to twenty-one points—his season high! Syracuse then picked up a road win over Rochester, 94–88, on Saturday, February 5, before heading home the following night to face New York. The "Red Hot" Johnny Kerr, who dropped in twelve points, began an eight-game double-digit scoring streak, averaging seventeen points per game. In a close contest, the Nats squeaked out a victory, 77–75. Guard George King also dispatched eight field goals and five free throws on his way to twenty-one points.

The "Big Apple" played host to a division rivalry on Tuesday, February 8, as the Nats took on the Celtics—a team vulnerable away from "The Hub." While the partisan crowd delighted in a Boston loss, 115–88, turnabout is indeed fair play. Back in Boston the following night, a 104–94 loss befell Syracuse. Even with the win, and their slew of solid forwards and great guards, Boston still had one major problem: they didn't have a guy who could get them the ball—no great center, yet.

Syracuse next began a three-game home stand beginning Thursday, February 10, against Minneapolis. In the first of five straight wins for the team, Syracuse overpowered the Lakers, 85–81; Milwaukee, 92–66; Rochester, 88–87; Milwaukee, 82–81; and Boston, 107–93.

"Syracuse had a good team that year," recalls Arnie Risen. "As a team, we [Rochester] were having a bad year. Dolph Schayes and Red Kerr make any team great! Remember, Al Cervi left Rochester to coach Syracuse, so there was no love between Al and Les. While Les wanted to beat everyone, he tried extra hard to beat them [Syracuse]."

But in Philadelphia, the Nats lost to the Warriors, 110–86. The short streak had ended. It was then back-to-back (road and then home) games against New York—the Nats taking the first, 80–78, and the second, 104–84. On the road, Nats guard Dick Farley dropped sixteen points, while Schayes sank twenty-eight at home.

In New York, the Nats would lose a neutral court heartbreaker to the Celtics, 97–95, before heading back home for two quick victories to close

SYRACUSE NATIONALS

1954–55: THE PLAYERS

DOLPH SCHAYES **; 18.5 PPG; 887 TRB; 1333
TP; 422 FG; 1103 FGA; 489 FT; .833 FT%;
209 P-TP;167 P-FGA; 60 P-FG; 48 P-PF
PAUL SEYMOUR **; 2950 MP; 483 A; 410 P-MP;
75 P-A
RED ROCHA **; 41.8 P-FG%
RED KERR ** (R); 41.9 FG%
EARL LLOYD **; 283 PF
GEORGE KING
BILLY KENVILLE
DICK FARLEY (R)
CONNIE SIMMONS
JIM TUCKER (R)—only player not to play in all 11 P-G.
WALLY OSTERKORN
BILL GABOR—played in only three games during season.

COACH: AL CERVI

* listed in order by PPG; statistic(s) alongside name
indicate team leader; ** played all 72 games and scored
over 10 PPG; (R) = rookie; *Italic* = did not appear in
playoffs; **Bold** = All-Star; P- = playoffs.

Source: Team Records; some sources may vary.

Coach Cervi finished first in the Eastern Division...won the Eastern Finals (3-1) versus Boston...won the Finals (4-3) versus Fort Wayne...season record identical to Fort Wayne at 43-29, .597...won Eastern division by five games over Knickerbockers...had two seven-game winning streaks during season...scored 120 points against Boston on 12/9/54...had one streak of four straight losses...both Schayes and Seymour had over 1,000 FGA during regular season...team averaged 93.1 PPG during regular season and 97.2 during playoffs...King and Seymour combined for 137 assists during playoffs... outstanding 586 P-TRB!

1954–55 SEASON	G	FG	FT	PTS
	72	2418	1870	6706
PLAYOFFS (7-4)	11	356	357	1069

out the month: Rochester, 97–83, and Philadelphia, 105–77. Paul Seymour posted twenty-four points against Philly, his February high. A very different team, now 37-26, would roar into March.

MARCH 1955

When Sinclair Lewis—no relation to Fred Lewis (SU coach, 1962–68)—said, "Winter is not a season, it's an occupation," it must have been in reference to basketball in Central New York. As the college schedule drew to a close on the hill, basketball coach Marc Guley had been fully engaged for months with a team that finished 10-11 following a victory over Canisius. Dispensation came in the form of the team's leading scorer, Vinnie Cohen, who averaged 15.8 PPG; Guley was a mere two seasons removed from guiding Syracuse University to its first NCAA tournament berth (1956–57), while Cohen was being eyed by the Nats.

The Nationals concluded a seven-game win streak by beating Philadelphia at home on Sunday, March 6, 107–101. That stretch also included back-to-back road victories against Fort Wayne, a victory over the Knickerbockers (March 1), 105–102, and a close win over Milwaukee, 99–96. Production continued to flow: Johnny "Red" Kerr averaged more than seventeen points per game over eight games, George King scored twenty-two points (his season high) against Fort Worth and the ever impressive Schayes dropped thirty-one points against the Knickerbockers.

The final week of the season included three losses, however: Rochester, 100–97 (March 9); Minneapolis, 96–93 (March 10); and Milwaukee, 77–76 (March 13); Syracuse managed only one win at home against Fort Wayne, 112–92, on Saturday, March 12. Notwithstanding the final week, an impressive, if not intimidating, Syracuse team concluded their regular term, 43-29.

Contributing double-digit marks in every game this month was Paul Seymour; he and Schayes both broke the one-thousand-point season plateau. Seymour also led the team in assists with 483. Schayes and the "always at the right place at the right time" Earl Lloyd also dominated the boards. As expected, Schayes, too, landed the team free throw percentage mark at .833. Johnny "Red" Kerr took field goal percentage honors with .419.

THE EASTERN DIVISION FINALS

The division finals began at home on Tuesday, March 22, against Boston, and although the Nats were not new to the playoffs, this "just felt different." Aware of just how difficult winning would be at the Garden, the team believed that the only *real* answer was to win at home first! Picking up a pair of victories, 110–100 and 116–110, the Nats did precisely that.

If "Red's Boys" were the putative champions, it needed to be buttressed at home on Sunday, March 26. In one of the most exhausting battles of the season, a 100–97 overtime loss befell Syracuse. A fan yelled to a court departing Cervi, "It's over!" His response, audible to those nearby: "Like hell it is!" Unyielding, the Nats took to the parquet floor again on Sunday, putting a quietus to Boston, 110–94. Syracuse had won the Eastern Division Finals (3-1)! The sound of the steel grinding on the elevated tracks on Causeway Street, outside of the Garden, never seemed louder or more gratifying.

THE LEAGUE FINALS

Fort Wayne was a city named after General "Mad" Anthony Wayne, whose sobriquet was in tremendous contrast to Fred Zollner's Pistons; however, a commonality shared by both was an understanding that experience garnered success. The team's triumphs were attributed to their veteran players and a stalwart owner. A confident lot, they were not intimidated by Syracuse or any adversary. But even the underpinnings of success can have its distractions. Having guided his 43-29 team past the Minneapolis Lakers in three games to capture the West, Piston's Coach Charlie Eckman was still viewed by his own players as "a work in progress." As a former referee and in his initial coaching season, he was widely criticized for his inexperience—a media prey for denunciation. But in his defense, Eckman had also made some quality decisions, including starting George Yardley, who had been relegated to an inferior role.

The Pistons were brimming with talent, beginning with the competent hands of Larry Foust and erudite athleticism of Yardley; both compiled more than one thousand points during the season. They were also enhanced by five skilled veterans, all of whom scored more than five hundred points: the durable Mel Hutchins, marksman Max Zaslofsky, an imperishable Frankie "Flash" Brian and virtuoso Andy Phillip. The trio of Foust, Yardley and Phillip had all made, and started for, the West All-Star team, paradoxically coached by Eckman. Like a scene out of *Beowulf*, the select team lost, 100–91, in front of more than fifteen thousand fans—inside Madison Square Garden—to an East team coached by none other than Al Cervi of Syracuse.

With little doubt that he could outsmart—or, as it is now termed, "outcoach"—arbiter Eckman, Cervi, in his authoritarian capacity, was optimistic. Frankly speaking, Cervi doubted that he would have ever faced Eckman in the finals, having instead predicted either Minneapolis or Rochester—both of whom were playing for the rights to meet Fort Wayne. Although the "Mikan-less" Lakers defeated Rochester, their effervescence had diminished, losing 3-1 to the Pistons.

Ironically, much of the event's early media coverage centered on another sport: bowling. You see, Fred Zollner was also backing the Allen

County War Memorial Coliseum as a Midwest business focal point—the site caught the attention of the ABC (American Bowling Congress), the nation's largest bowling tour. In a bit of skittles serendipity, the hardwood floor of the Coliseum was removed and replaced by bowling alleys. The Pistons had to find a new home, which they did, at the Indianapolis State Fairgrounds Coliseum, more than one hundred miles southwest of Fort Wayne. When told of the bowling debacle, Biasone—no stranger to falling pins himself—just smiled; however, inside he actually felt sorry for Zollner, who had played many games at Fort Wayne's North Side High School while attempting to convince the city to build an arena.

Syracuse had a *clear* home advantage—having won seven out of nine during regular play—as the Pistons had not won inside the War Memorial this season. Naturally, the press had a field day with Zollner's blunder—not only did the league finals feature the two smallest markets, but the priority was also "pins over pop shots."

The series began at home on Thursday, March 31, with the Nats picking up the opener 86–82. Red Rocha realized eight field goals and three foul shots for nineteen points, Paul Seymour dropped in seventeen points and Earl Lloyd scored an impressive twelve. During the fourth quarter, and down four, Coach Cervi had inserted Dick Farley into the game, and his quick four points really turned the momentum—a delightful dose of maturity and machination.

During game two (April 2), it became clear to everyone in Syracuse that the Pistons would not relent. They were not intimidated by their presence inside the Nats home nor by their opponent. The Pistons were going to make Syracuse work for the title; the Nats had led by eleven points at the half, but with thirty seconds left, the Pistons cut it to 85–84. In a nerve-racking half-minute interlude that prefaced the Nationals' second victory, Syracuse persevered, 87–84. Dolph Schayes took charge with twenty-four points, and Johnny Kerr came alive for seventeen points—he had scored only eight in the previous game.

Up two games, cautious optimism prevailed over cynicism, as Syracuse made their way to Indianapolis on Sunday. But buoyancy can have its misgivings. Despite Rocha and Schayes scoring twenty-one points each for Syracuse, they couldn't halt Fort Wayne's offensive attack. Mel Hutchins dominated the boards for the Pistons while scoring twenty-two points, and Andy Phillip conducted a clinic on his way to tally sixteen. Fort Wayne took the solid victory, 96–89. It was an inexorable statement made by a potent and deft Pistons team. For the 3,200 fans in attendance, it was a bit of a reprieve.

Nationals v. Pistons—Indianapolis

Sunday, April 3, 1955—Game Three
Syracuse Nationals v. Fort Wayne Pistons

89   -   96

Tuesday, April 5, 1955—Game Four
Syracuse Nationals v. Fort Wayne Pistons

102   -   109

Thursday, April 7, 1955—Game Five
Syracuse Nationals v. Fort Wayne Pistons

71   -   74

A summary of the 1954–55 playoff road games, held in Indianapolis, at the Indiana State Fair Coliseum (Pepsi Coliseum). *Elizabeth Baker.*

An emotionally charged Fort Wayne team greeted Syracuse on Tuesday, April 5. While foreshadowed by the Nationals, the robustness of its delivery was not—it was a veritable cascade of confidence. Even the press was raving over what they had witnessed, calling it their best basketball all season. Seven players in double figures led the evenhanded Pistons' attack to a 109–102 victory. The Nats' problematic shooting—the team hit just 32 of 103 shots from the field—was as disconcerting as it was defective. Schayes, who had twenty-eight points in the game, even marveled at the proficiency of his opponents, who took an eighteen-point lead at one point. The series was now tied, 2-2.

In the face of the loss, an intrepid Syracuse team took to the hardwood on Thursday, April 7. During the third period, as the momentum shifted in favor of the Nats, an angry fan unleashed a tirade that included a chair flying over the heads on the Syracuse bench and onto the floor; an inebriated myrmidon, one might suspect, but nobody was certain. It sounded like an explosion, Paul Seymour would later recall. The diminutive man responsible for the incident then exchanged a few unpleasant commands with Syracuse's George King before being led away.

The suspense-filled evening then witnessed Syracuse with the ball, down by a point. With a mere twelve seconds remaining, guard Dick Farley—no stranger to Indiana basketball—took command and set himself up for a short-range shot at the nine-second mark. The crowd of 4,111 Hoosiers watched as Farley's shot caressed the rim but did not fall into the basket; instead, it fell into the hands of Pistons guard Frank Brian. Syracuse immediately fouled Brian, but by then the clock had ticked down to a single second remaining. As the Nats watched Brian sink two shots from the charity stripe and bring the final score to 74–71, their hearts skipped a beat. Five days ago, everything was working in their favor; now it appeared that nothing could go right.

Unhappy fans, incensed by the remarks flung by King, were determined not to allow Syracuse to leave the building after the game. A skirmish between Nats coach Al Cervi and an irate fan found the latter shirtless; however, that would not be all, as King was later charged with making threatening statements in connection with the chair-throwing incident. The man who had thrown the chair—an off-duty policeman—later obtained a warrant against the Syracuse player. Far from recalcitrant, King concluded the event with an apology.

Back home, down a game and momentum clearly *not* in their favor—after three straight losses, how could it be—the Nats took center court on Saturday, April 9. Certainly here, ratiocination would now prevail over illogical sentiment, or so one might hope. In an atmosphere tense with undercurrents, Fort Wayne took an immediate lead and extended it by as much as ten points in the first half; harsh gesticulations, directed at the Pistons, were as common as cars along Montgomery Street.

In the second period, it wasn't long before the Nats' Wally Osterkorn and the Pistons' Don Meineke traded punches. In retaliation for the Hoosier hoodlum's debacle of the previous game, Syracuse fans spilled out onto the floor. After police restored order, somewhat reluctantly, of course, the game continued. With just over four minutes to play, the Nats took the lead with an Earl Lloyd set shot. At the ninety-second mark, the Pistons tied it at 103 apiece. A Johnny Kerr jumper, a Farley tap-in and some free throws helped secure the 109–104 victory.

Now, if you will pardon the elaboration—presumptuous by no means—let me expound. The intensity of this contest had never before been witnessed during league finals, and it wasn't over! Not a single player was playing for himself; they were all playing for the good of their team, their franchise and their fans—it was, by all accounts, a felicitous act of unselfishness.

For both cities, the event *now* meant even more; it was a small-market ratification—the perfect league "win-win scenario."

GAME SEVEN

Standing outside of the War Memorial Auditorium on this beautiful Easter Sunday, you could hear the bells ringing at the Cathedral of the Immaculate Conception (St. Mary's Catholic Church) over on East Onondaga Street and even more chimes from an opposite direction. More than one prayer, on this day, would ask God to bless our team, "Danny's Boys." Tipoff inside, on *our* court, was set for 3:30 p.m.

The Pistons, determined to take the crowd out of the equation—as if this has ever been possible in Syracuse—ran up a big lead, as large as seventeen points at one point (41–24) during the second period. Just think: a year earlier, the game would have been over, stalled by Fort Wayne on their way to victory. But now a clock—a 24-second variety—prevented such a strategy and enhanced the rules of engagement. In an action he had perfected during the season, Cervi then pulled Seymour and King in favor of Kenville and Farley. A momentum changer, Cervi would later recall, and it worked. Syracuse rallied. A pensive Biasone, sitting on the bench, watched every move from his gifted coach.

By halftime it was 53–47, advantage Syracuse. But momentum was shifting toward Fort Wayne. With about a minute and a half remaining, the Pistons went up, 90–89. Integrating all accounts, allow me to take you there now.

With the series tied three to three, basketball history was being made here in Syracuse, New York, as thousands of fans were packed wall-to-wall inside the War Memorial. "Everywhere I looked, people were on the edge of their seats," claimed Ann Meyer. "I kept looking upward into the rafters overhead, where people were perched almost over the court, yelling downward. It was overwhelming!"

Schayes at the line for two made them both; Syracuse now led, 91–90.

Brian brought the ball down court and passed to Yardley. Guarded by Lloyd, Yardley passed to Phillip, who tried to get the ball inside to Foust. Seven seconds on the clock as the ball was passed to Brian; then it was back to Yardley. Yardley, sensing room, jumped, shot and missed, but a foul was called on George King of Syracuse. "Yardley was our best player," commented Piston Bob Houbregs, "so we were running a play to get him the best shot possible." As for Syracuse, Schayes confirmed it was not an intentional foul against Yardley.

"I kept staring at the clock, watching the time," spoke Ben DiFrancisco. "Every second felt like a minute. When King fouled Yardley, I didn't know what to think. It must have been the right move, at least that's what I thought."

"The Bird," George Yardley, was at the line for one; it was good! We were tied, folks, 91 all!

"I was just a kid," spoke John Kerrigan. "Every woman in the place had a hat on, and I was sitting behind the biggest one. This gal never moved the entire game. I kept trying to squeeze a look around her but couldn't. Finally, I stood, with about a minute left."

Fifty-nine seconds remained in this game-seven finale. It was Lloyd to King, who drove but saw no daylight. So it was back to Lloyd, with fifty seconds remaining. Lloyd looked and then passed it back to King. Eight seconds left on the shot clock; Lloyd would have to hurry—he shot, it was no good. Rebound by Phillip of the Pistons—still 91–91 with thirty-six seconds to go and twenty seconds on the shot clock.

"Oh God," remembered Ann Meyer. "I jumped out of my seat, then sat back down quickly, what was I doing, I thought. Wait. What were they doing?"

Andy Phillip of the Pistons was now in command as his team set, looking, looking…he spotted Yardley, who passed back to Phillip. Looking for Foust, Phillip found him, but he couldn't take the shot, so it was over to Yardley. He would have to hurry…underneath he went. There was a whistle; looked like traveling and it was. Traveling was called. Traveling with 18…17… seconds left. The players on the Pistons bench just couldn't believe it. (Many would later claim favoritism toward Syracuse.) "It was argued," claimed Bob Houbregs, "but to no avail." Yardley couldn't believe it either, as he was indicating that the ball was batted away before he picked it up. The referees claimed that he shuffled his feet getting to the ball. It was just so hard to see from most vantage points. Syracuse wisely called a time-out.

The Syracuse crowd was just beside themselves, people fidgeting, looking around, looking down—searching the crowd for a reprieve to the tension. Biasone looked at Cervi, looked down and then back at Cervi. Everywhere you looked, the game was playing out on the faces of those watching.

The 24-second clock was now "off," folks. It was only the master clock above that counted. Syracuse tried to position themselves for the last shot; seventeen seconds to go and we were tied. The crowd was screaming as the Nationals' King inbounded (bench sideline—about four feet from half-court) to Kerr (hugging the sideline), then Kerr back to King (nearly identical position); the time was down to twelve seconds. King with a one-bounce dribble back into the half-court corner, where he was trapped. A whistle was blown by the referee directly behind King. It was hard to hear above the crowd. Yes, Brian, whose hands were around King's neck reaching for the ball, had fouled George King—the Nats' best ball handler and the worst foul shooter. "Brian intentionally fouled King," Schayes later recalled; however, some differ in opinion. A fervent Cervi could not watch King; he turned away and caught Biasone in his peripheral vision. Both, they would later acknowledge, were praying.

"I looked at Cervi from where we were sitting," spoke Anthony Rossi, "and I swear he said, 'Give us the ball, Lord,' or something like that." It was just overwhelming at this point; the crowd, with some hands clasped in prayer, could not believe what they were witnessing.

It was a single-shot foul for King, with twelve seconds remaining. Twelve seconds! Incredible! The Syracuse police were now positioning themselves courtside, even surrounding the Fort Wayne bench—the team was so involved with the game that they didn't realize that the authorities had arrived; there would be no monkey business here in Syracuse. King aimed and shot the one-hander—it was good, 92–91, Syracuse! Fort Wayne would have one

Syracuse, N.Y.—1955: The World Champions of Basketball Syracuse Nationals pose for a team portrait. Front Row (L-R): Dick Farley, Billy Kenville; Center Row: Earl Lloyd, Captain Paul Seymour, Head Coach Al Cervi, George King Jim Tucker; Rear Row: President Daniel Biasone, Wally Osterkorn, Business Manager Bob Sexton, Dolph Schayes, John Kerr, Billy Gabor Red Rocha, Trainer Art Van Auken in Syracuse, New York, in 1955. Copyright Notice: Copyright 1965 NBAE. *Photo by Dick Raphael/NBAE via Getty Images.*

more shot as the ball was inbound (at twelve seconds) to Phillip, who took three and a half dribbles to go beyond half-court; we're at nine seconds. He looked to the corner. Paul Seymour was just all over Phillip, and as he reversed his dribble to turn away from his defender (about a step from the top of the key), King had left his man to double-team Phillip and caught him completely by surprise. The ball was stolen—stolen by big George King, who dribbled a couple steps toward the baseline before reversing direction, three…two…one. When asked if this was a clean steal, Piston player Houbregs responded, "Debatable—could have gone either way." The game was over. Syracuse had won. Danny Biasone, you have your championship! Syracuse won, 92–91!

"Like others, my friend Gary and I ran out onto the court and just began screaming," recalled Jeffrey Gleason. "We just patted everyone on the back. Wow, what a game!" Paul Seymour would later recall how he felt he had gotten away with a foul by aggressively bumping Phillip. Many in attendance felt bad for the Pistons, but even Biasone couldn't escape a satisfying grin. The humble victor was also quick to credit his invention, which he felt aided in the victory, believing in his heart that had the shot clock not been there, the Pistons—up by seventeen at one point—could have stalled their way to victory.

In a poetic opus, "It was two great owners with two great teams, hometown hearts living hardwood dreams."

Chapter 5

A BIG-LEAGUE TEAM IN A SMALL TOWN, 1955–1959

A championship must be defended in order for it to be retained. For the five sets of Syracuse shoulders on the court, and their support system, no task could have been more overwhelming. Champions, particularly in professional sports, need motivation more than just another title, the revenue it provides or the security it can bring—they need something above and beyond wining, something on the other side of themselves. Often that stimulus is very personal, as the few who have accomplished the task claim it must be. Al Cervi had to find that in his players, extract it and place it on the hardwood.

While the owners, coaches and players were still acclimating to running their lives in 24-second segments, during a season that was too long for some and not long enough for others, the league watched as the Hawks relocated from Milwaukee to St. Louis, Missouri; the growing pains were clearly not over.

The 1955–56 Season: Valiant

"The world champions made a valiant effort to retain their title" is precisely how team management would assess the season—most of the more than 140,000 witnesses inside the War Memorial during the event would concur.

Gone from the championship team were Bill Gabor, Wally Osterkorn and Connie Simmons, while the Nats added to their roster first-round draft pick

SYRACUSE HARDWOOD HERO

Edward James Conlin

Position: Forward - Guard
Height: 6-5
Weight: 200 lbs.
Born: September 2, 1933
High School: Saint Michael's in Brooklyn, New York
College: Fordham University
SYR Uniform #: 8 - 11

Began career with Syracuse, 1955–56…played his final game with the Warriors during the 1961–62 season…tough and dependable, "Ed" scored over 500 points during his rookie season…played over 250 games for Syracuse…gathered over 2,300 career rebounds…selected by the Nationals in the 1955 league draft.

Ed was traded by the Nationals to the Pistons for George Yardley on February 13, 1959…later coached men's basketball at Fordham University…played with Wilt Chamberlain in the famous 100-point game, March 2, 1962, at Hersheypark Arena…averaged 10.1 PPG in his NBA career.

CAREER NBA	G	FG	FT	PTS
	486	1862	1167	4891

Ed Conlin from Fordham University. Players who were drafted but would not play included Don Schlundt, Jack Sallee, Frank Ehmann, Mal Duffy, Cliff Dwyer, Ed Galvin, Stan Glowaski, Russ Lawler, Marty Satalino and Ron Tomsic. The titleholder's primary defense would be Schayes, King, Kerr, Lloyd, Seymour and Rocha.

A modest, but dedicated, crowd of 3,789 attended the season opener at home against a familiar adversary, Fort Wayne. Naturally, expectations were high on this Saturday, November 5. Although the Nats would begin with an exciting 114–113 victory over the Pistons, by the end of the month they were 6-6, never having won consecutive games. While the scoring pace picked up in December, the team having even topped the century mark six times, the frequency of wins did not; standing firm at 14-14, the Nats entered 1956.

Rochester played host to the All-Star Game on January 24, with the West beating the East 108–94. The Nationals' contingent of Schayes and Kerr, who combined for only eighteen points, looked fatigued. The West was led by game MVP Bob Pettit, who chalked up a game-high twenty points.

A dismal January witnessed both a four- and three-game losing streak. Coach Cervi finally got the momentum to shift in February, as the Nats won three in a row, lost three in a row and then won seven straight games—four of which were over the Knickerbockers. But the club remained below .500 in February and finished the regular season that way, at 35-37.

The Nationals' distributed and durable attack—only two players did *not* score more than five hundred points during the season—was led by a steadfast Dolph Schayes (20.4 PPG); all but three players—Paul Seymour, Ed Conlin and Jim Tucker—appeared in all seventy-two games. If this club was going to lose, Coach Al Cervi thought, they would do so as a team, and they did; the Nats lost nine times to Philly and eight times to Boston.

Finishing tied for third—or last, depending on your perspective—in their division felt like an understatement. The team scored 96.9 points per game but gave the exact amount back. If a champion is defined as someone who gets up when he can't, then the Nats got up half the time. Naturally, some redemption came in the form of an East Division tiebreaking win over the Knickerbockers and even more when the team took Boston 2-1 in the semis. While "repeat" seemed incomprehensible, it was on the minds of some, but the loss, 3-2, versus Philadelphia in the division finals crushed that dream. For Cervi, the "V" in "valiant" (the retrospective adjective, used in team-issued correspondence to forever account for the season) meant victory, an idea that his team, he would reflect, had forsaken too often.

The league's tenth season ended with Philadelphia winning the title, beating Fort Wayne four games to one in the finals.

STATS AND FACTS

Deciding to hand out a Most Valuable Player trophy for the first time, the league's Bob Pettit of St. Louis becomes the first recipient—a well-deserved honor for the points (1,849) and rebound (1,164) leader. Rookie of the Year honors went to Maurice Stokes of Rochester.

The draft was held on April 30, 1956, as eight league teams took turns selecting amateur U.S. college basketball players. In each round, the teams selected in reverse order of their win-loss record in the previous season, except for the defending champion and runner-up, who were assigned the last two picks on each round. Now, as anyone who follows professional basketball will tell you, anything and everything can happen on draft day.

In what would later be acknowledged as one of the most pivotal days in league history, Boston, in an inferior draft position, managed to acquire three future Hall of Famers: Bill Russell (drafted by St. Louis in round one—number two overall—and traded to Boston for Ed Macauley and Cliff Hagan), K.C. Jones (round two) and Tom Heinsohn (Boston's territorial pick). Auerbach, having set his sights on prime target Bill Russell (University of San Francisco), had to skillfully maneuver himself into the proper position to obtain his treasure. This meant fulfilling the needs of both Rochester, who had the first pick, and St. Louis, who had the second—either of whom would likely choose Russell. Terms of engagement, as it was later confirmed in John Feinstein's book *Let Me Tell a Story: A Lifetime in the Game,* even called for Auerbach having team owner Walter A. Brown, who was also president of the Ice Capades, call Lester Harrison, the owner in Rochester, and discreetly offer him local ice show appearances in lieu of Russell consideration.

Speaking of diplomacy, at the request of the State Department, the Syracuse Nationals went abroad as goodwill ambassadors—"Dribblers without Borders." The team traveled thirty thousand miles, visiting Iceland, Germany, Iran, Lebanon, Italy, Spain and Egypt. It was another reflection of just how popular the game had become.

THE 1956–57 SEASON: A PESSIMIST'S PROGNOSTICATIONS

Less than twenty days from the improbable (a perfect game in a baseball World Series), Al Cervi, who did not include himself in the forecast, released to the public his "Predictions (and Fabrications)." In the manifesto, he professed: "Any coach who is asked to predict how his team will fare in the league is bound to become a pessimist. When you talk about beating the best basketball teams in the world, you've got to be a pessimist. It's that hard." Cervi then continued with some team assessments: "The Warriors," he thought, "defending champions are the team to beat, but they will miss Tom Gola." (They finished third.) Cervi also predicted Boston to contend (they would win the league crown) and the Hawks to relinquish the Western title to Fort Wayne (they would) and felt that Minneapolis "lacked the depth" to contend (they tied for first). Prophecy now comfortably in print, the Nostradamus of the hardwood sought his own destiny.

A typical professional basketball team has few, if any, championship years, many regular seasons and a handful, or more, of "transitional terms"—the latter formerly synonymous with "a lousy year" but now being referred to under a more politically correct locution: "a rebuilding period." The "Cervi Years" were now drawing to a close, and the "Seymour Saga" was about to begin. Twelve games into the season, a conversion was made. In 495 NBA games, Al Cervi had compiled a winning record of 294-201 and had given Syracuse a league title—not bad for a hard-nosed kid from the streets of Buffalo.

Central New York Basketball, Inc., "the team the fans own," was precisely that in 1956. In addition to the tremendous individual support the team experienced, many businesses also had a stake in the team, including the Carrier Corporation Employee Association; Central Restaurant Supply, Inc.; Collins & Company, Inc.; Abe Cooper-Syracuse, Inc.; Hotel Onondaga; Hotel Syracuse, Inc.; L. Johnson & Company; Netherland Company; and Station WNDR. The organization beneath Biasone was also stocked with talent, including Robert W. Sexton, business manager and publicity director; Art Van Auken, trainer; Joe Weber, official scorer; Ralph Esposito, official timer; Billy Hassett, 24-second timer; Whitey Anderson, statistician; Jim McKechnie, broadcaster; Jerry Walser, ticket manager; Joe Pitonzo, auditor; and Virginia Chookasian, secretary—a proficient mix of hardwood personnel!

SYRACUSE HARDWOOD HERO

Alfred A. "Al" Bianchi

Position: Guard
Height: 6-3
Weight: 185 lbs.
Born: March 26, 1932, in Long Island City, New York
College: Bowling Green State University
SYR Uniform #: 16 - 24

Began career with the Nationals, 1956–57...played his final game with Philadelphia during the 1965–66 season...durable, defensive and accurate, "Al" was a playmaker on the Syracuse hardwood...played seven seasons for the Nats...he played every game of the 1958–59 and 1961–62 seasons...was drafted by Minneapolis in 1954 and then sold to Syracuse in 1956.

Al was hired as the Bulls' first assistant coach...served as the first head coach for Seattle (1967–69)...coached Washington (1969–70) and the Virginia Squires (1970–76) of the ABA...named 1970–71 ABA Coach of the Year...served as the General Manager for New York from 1987 to 1991...always a fan favorite!

CAREER NBA	G	FG	FT	PTS
	687	2212	1126	5550

SYRACUSE HARDWOOD HERO

Robert William Harrison

Position: Guard
Height: 6-1
Weight: 190 lbs.
Born: August 12, 1927
High School: Woodward in Toledo, Ohio
College: University of Michigan
SYR Uniform #: 3

Began career with Minneapolis, 1949–50...played his final game with Syracuse during the 1957–58 season...played in 1956 All-Star game...an aggressive defender, "Bob" was sold by the Hawks to the Nationals on December 2, 1956...played for two seasons with Syracuse...longtime friend of Nats' coach Paul Seymour...solid one-hand set shot.

Tiger scored over 500 points in each of his two seasons with the Nats... durable player who competed in the entire 1957–58 season...he was sold by the Lakers to Milwaukee (St. Louis) in December 1953...former Michigan All-American, he later coached at Kenyon College and Harvard.

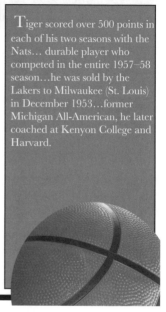

CAREER NBA	G	FG	FT	PTS
	615	1782	854	4418

Speaking of community interaction, imagine this: "I attended Syracuse Central High School," speaks Bill Martin, "a stone's throw from the War Memorial. On a couple of occasions the high school basketball players actually scrimmaged against the Nats."

Missing from this year's scorecard were Dick Farley, Billy Kenville, George King and Red Rocha, while the Nats added to their roster rookie Forest Able, rookie Al Bianchi, veteran Bob Harrison (sold by the Hawks), free agent Larry Hennessy, first-round draft pick Joe Holup, rookie Bob Hopkins, Togo Palazzi (sold by Boston), rookie Jim Ray, Don Savage and free agent Bob Schafer. Players who were drafted but would not play included Willie Bergines, Colgate's Milt Graham, the very tall Swede Halbrook (who wouldn't join the team until the 1960–61 season), Paul Judson, Dick Julio, LeMoyne College standout Dick Kenyon, Jim McLaughlin, Jess Roh, Chuck Rolles and Chester Webb. Schayes, Colin, Kerr, Lloyd, Harrison and Bianchi led the Syracuse strike force.

The Nationals opened the season with three straight victories followed by five consecutive losses. A win against Philadelphia, on Sunday, November 18, stopped the bleeding but only briefly—the Nats would lose their next

SYRACUSE HARDWOOD HERO

Robert M. Hopkins

Position: Center-Forward
Height: 6-8
Weight: 205 lbs.
Born: November 3, 1934 in Jonesboro, Louisiana
College: Grambling State University
SYR Uniform #: 9

Began career with the Nationals, 1956–57…after four seasons, played his final game with the club during the 1959–60 season…selected by Syracuse in the tenth round (seventy-fifth pick) of the 1956 league draft…excellent free throw shooter…scored over 500 points for three consecutive seasons with the Nats…received military deferment for being over height limit.

Bob coached with Seattle during part of the 1977–78 season…appeared in 273 games for Syracuse…averaged 8.2 points per game during four seasons as a member of the Nats…logged over 5,000 playing minutes as a Syracuse player…had a career .761 FT percentage.

CAREER NBA	G	FG	FT	PTS
	273	854	529	2237

SYRACUSE HARDWOOD HERO

Togo Anthony Palazzi

Position: Forward - Guard
Height: 6-4
Weight: 205 lbs.
Born: August 8, 1932, in Union City, New Jersey
High School: Union Hill in Union City, NJ
College: College of the Holy Cross
SYR Uniform #: 6 - 17

Began career with Boston, 1954–55…played his final game with the Nationals during the 1959–60 season…Togo was an accurate free throw shooter…scored over 500 points in each full season with the Nats…appeared in over 200 games for Syracuse…sold by Boston to the Nats in November 1956.

Togo was captain of the Holy Cross Crusaders team that won the 1954 NIT Championship—he was named MVP of the tournament…prior to playing in Boston, Red Auerbach tried to recruit Palazzi to play at Duke University…placed on the inactive list by Boston to make room for Bill Russell…a fan favorite.

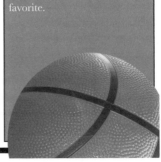

CAREER NBA	G	FG	FT	PTS
	324	937	508	2382

six games. Following a 114–99 road loss to the Celtics, the third in the six-game slide, Cervi had had enough. Player-coach Paul Seymour took over on Tuesday, November 27, as Syracuse took on Rochester in New York City—the team lost 90–82. Seymour's first win as a coach came on Sunday, December 2, when the Nationals defeated the Knickerbockers at home, 110–100. But by the end of the month, the struggling team could only post a record of 10-17.

The turning point for the club came in January as they managed to compile both a three- and six-game winning streak to take them to just under .500 (23-24) at month's end. On Tuesday, January 15, in Boston, the East overtook the West, 109–97, in the annual All-Star gala. Ambassador Schayes represented Syracuse and, like the game's MVP Bob Cousy, served beneath Lord Auerbach of the East.

Momentum continued in the club's favor as they reached the break-even mark on February 21. Seymour and company then finished strong to close out the season, 38-34 (.528). A Syracuse second-place finish six games behind Boston meant meeting the Warriors in the division semis, which they took handily (2-0). It was now on to Boston in the East Finals.

The Celtics exhibited no mercy and swept the Nationals in three straight games on their way to a league championship (which would be the first of what would be eleven championships in thirteen years). Much of the praise for the season went to Auerbach—exactly the way he liked it.

Arnold Jacob Auerbach was born on September 20, 1917, in the Williamsburg section of Brooklyn. Since his days at Eastern District High School, he wanted to play basketball, but given that this was the mid-1930s, his only options were barnstorming or regional college ball; little recruiting meant tryouts. Legendary coach Nat Holman wanted Red to play for him at City College; the only problem were his grades, too low to meet the requirements. So Auerbach ended up at Seth Low Junior College in Brooklyn—a conduit for Columbia talent; instead of becoming a Lion, Auerbach ended up at George Washington University. It was a different world then; for example, when northeastern teams played below the Mason-Dixon line, like in Washington, D.C., their black players remained at home because they knew they wouldn't be allowed to play in segregated cities.

Auerbach began coaching basketball in 1941 at the St. Albans School and Roosevelt High School in "D.C.," the place he called home. Two years later, he joined the U.S. Navy and coached its basketball team in Norfolk. It was there in Tidewater where he caught the eye of Washington millionaire Mike Uline, who hired him to instruct the Washington Capitols in the newly founded Basketball Association of America (BAA). Stability in the coaching ranks finally came in 1950 with a phone call from Celtics owner Walter A. Brown.

On paper, the Nats were actually a far worse team—they gave up more points than they scored, and most mathematical formulas spoke to a team who should have finished well under .500 for the season. On the upside, seven players finished with more than five hundred points: Schayes (1,617), Conlin, Kerr, Lloyd and Harrison, along with rookies Bianchi and Holup. An inexorable Schayes posted a near perfect FT percentage of .904!

NATS NUGGETS

In a sport often defined via personal confrontations—"Bird v. Magic" or "Chamberlain v. Russell"—not enough has ever been said about "Sharman v. Schayes." These two gladiators, the finest two pair of eyes ever to take to the charity stripe, battled for the free throw percentage crown annually between 1951 and 1961. (Sharman played from 1950–51 to 1960–61.) Often separated by only a swing or two of the net, both athletes displayed an extraordinary level of commitment to their profession. For ten straight seasons, count 'em, the name Sharman, which appeared seven times, or Schayes, three times, was atop the charity circlet.

During this season, Sharman would take the title for the fifth straight year, and at a 90.5 mark—his first season above 90 percent! The MVP award went to his teammate, Bob Cousy, and the Rookie of the Year recipient was Tom Heinsohn, also from Boston.

We were now living in a Celtics world, whether the players liked it or not—the latter opinion being the most prevalent. One of those not shy about conveying his dissatisfaction with the "World According to Red" was rookie Al Bianchi, who was often given the task of guarding (or watching, depending on your perspective) the spectacular Bob Cousy. Coach Seymour often recounted telling Bianchi to put Cousy on his ass whenever he felt humiliated by the guard, which Bianchi welcomed and frequently did. (Cousy didn't recall the incidents when asked.) Syracuse fans loved it, as more often than not the upstate referees turned a blind eye to the occurrence.

Seymour's disdain for Red Auerbach (or Red "Drawback" or Red "On-our-back," as he referred to him) was not an uncommon competitive element. While it was Emerson who said, "Win as if you were used to it, lose as if you enjoyed it for a change," it was Auerbach who modified it to "Lose and you will be in for a change." The ironic thing, Coach Seymour would later tell me, was that this SOB (Auerbach) was just as arrogant before he began winning championships.

The next five seasons (1956–57 through 1960–61) would witness enormous league production gains: team averages included FGA (6,809 to 8,642), rebounds (4,494 to 5,789), FG percentages (38 percent to 41.5 percent) and PPG (99.6 to 118.1). The reason was simple: limited defensive play, along with an emphasis on speed and offense. Contrast this against today's game. As of 2009–2010 (eighty-two games): FGA (6,700), rebounds (3,421), FG percentage (.461) and PPG (100.4).

THE 1957–58 SEASON: SCHAYES DAYS

Only a few months removed from Senator John F. Kennedy's motivating speech at Syracuse University's 103rd Commencement, Danny Biasone stood alone looking out from the windows of the Eastwood Sports Center. He understood but perhaps couldn't accept that change was coming. The Pistons, a minor market team, relocated from Fort Wayne to Detroit, Michigan, and another team, the Royals—just a few miles west on the ultramodern New York State Thruway—relocated from Rochester to Cincinnati, Ohio. Biasone, he thought, owed it to *his* community, *his* friends, *his* players and *his* coach to remain faithful, irrevocable to change. Besides, he owed Paul (Seymour) a chance to work some Salt City magic.

Missing from last season's "transitional term" were Forest Able, Larry Hennessy, Jim Ray, Don Savage, Bob Schafer and Jim Tucker, while the Nats added to their roster guard Larry Costello from Niagara University (sold by the Warriors). Players who were drafted but would not play included George Bon Salle, Jim Morgan, Syracuse University standout Vince Cohen, Jerry Mallett, Frank Nimmo, Lyndon Lee, Dick Gaines, Cebe Price, Syracuse University legend Jim Brown, Colgate's Jack Nichols and Jim Weeks. The Nats would counter their opponents with Schayes (F-C), Costello (G), Kerr (C-F), Conlin (F-G), Harrison (G) and Bianchi (G).

The season opener was home, on Friday, October 25, against Philadelphia. Not since the opening of the 1953–54 season—also against Philly—had Syracuse witnessed such a powerful atmosphere. The crowd of 7,112 delighted in their team's performance. Coach Seymour had his club ready and it showed, as they won the game handily, 103–85. While the Nats were scoring points, the baskets didn't always fall their way, and by the end of November

SYRACUSE HARDWOOD LEGEND

Larry Ronald Costello

Position: Guard
Height: 6-1
Weight: 186 lbs.
Born: July 2, 1931, in Minoa, New York
High School: Minoa
College: Niagara University
SYR Uniform #: 15 - 6 - 21

Began career with Philly during the 1954–55 season...spent six seasons with the Nats...played his final game with Philadelphia during the 1967–68 season...scored over 500 points in nine consecutive seasons...named to 1958-1959-1960-1961-1962-1965 All-Star teams...led the league twice in FT percentage...an accurate and efficient shooter.

Larry was an outstanding league playmaker...took over as head coach of the expansion Bucks in 1968 and brought them to a league-best 66-16 mark in 1970–71, including a then league record twenty-game win streak...coached the Bulls for fifty-six games in 1978–79...last coaching job was at Utica College in the 1980s.

CAREER NBA	G	FG	FT	PTS
	706	3095	2432	8622

the team was 7-9. December started out with a three-game winning streak, followed later by another, bringing the club above .500, at 18-14.

The All-Star Game, played in St. Louis on Tuesday, January 21, saw the East dominate the West, 130–118. Dolph Schayes and Larry Costello represented an improving Nationals squad. Local hero Bob Pettit of the Hawks managed to pick up the game's MVP award.

Syracuse finished 41-31, eight games behind Boston, putting them second in the East. Momentum, which didn't appear in their favor, wasn't, as they lost in the division semis to the Warriors, 2-1. In retrospect, they were a squad that should have gone much deeper toward the championship—in truth they should have made it to the final game. They outscored their opposition and played better defense, and all but three players on the team scored more than five hundred points; three even scored above one thousand: Schayes (in perhaps his finest season, 24.9 PPG), Kerr and Costello.

Particularly impressive was Larry Costello, leading the team in field goal percentage while playing the second-most minutes; only Schayes played more at 2,918 minutes. Costello also emerged as a playmaker, a powerful point guard who contributed 317 assists, just under 100 more than Schayes, who had 224. He was aggressive, sometimes overly so, but not enough to get on the wrong side of Seymour, who even tolerated Costello leading the team in personal fouls (246).

Lawrence Ronald "Larry" Costello was born on July 2, 1931, in Minoa, New York. After playing at Niagara University, where he averaged 15 PPG, he was drafted by Philadelphia in 1954. He was later sold to Syracuse (1957), where he would stay until his retirement in 1965 from Philadelphia (aka Syracuse). Costello came back for the 1966–67 NBA season after new head coach (and former National) Alex Hannum told him that he needed a veteran point guard. But Costello ripped his Achilles tendon on January 6, 1967, forty-two games into the season and was replaced by Wali Jones; he did, however, come back to participate in the 1966–67 playoffs. He ended his career for the second and final time in 1968, having even been drafted by the expansion Bucks.

Milwaukee's only league championship (1971) may be Costello's coaching legacy, but he is beloved in Central New York for many reasons. First, for being a member of the Nationals; second, for beginning his coaching career at East Syracuse–Minoa High School—where he coached the boys' varsity basketball team to the state championship for the first time in school history; and finally, for his last coaching job, at Utica College in the 1980s. The school was making the transition from Division III to Division I as an independent. In his second year in Division I, the Pioneers were the seventh most improved team in the country based on their win-loss record. Costello's name often resurfaces during near perfect NBA shooting performances, as in 1961, while playing for the Nats, he hit thirty-two points without missing.

St. Louis won the league championship, beating Boston four games to two in the finals. Few would realize that it was the last time Red Auerbach coached a team who didn't finish the season by winning the championship, but even fewer would realize that it was Alex Hannum who would buttress both points of Auerbach's impressive streak—eight league titles!

Attendance last season at the Onondaga War Memorial, which seemed solid at just under 189,000 (fourth of eight teams), slipped to just over 112,000 (sixth of eight) during the year—this in the face of a quality term delivered by the Nationals.

NATS NOTATIONS

In a testament to player proficiency, league performance marks continued to be set as a player topped the two-thousand-point mark for the first time (George Yardley, Detroit, 2,001) and another grabbed more than 1,500 rebounds (Bill Russell, Boston, 1,564). Dolph Schayes of the Nationals also won his first efficiency crown from the charity stripe by posting a 90.4 mark.

Speaking of Yardley, the first "Bird" (his nickname was also "Yardbird") was playing his future team, Syracuse, on the final day of the regular season. Needing only twenty-five points to surpass the two-thousand-point plateau, the tenacious Yardley appeared predestined. Determined to suppress Bird's flight was Coach Seymour, who put his finest defenseman, Al Bianchi, on the six-foot-five forward. Unimpressed by the move, Bird buried Bianchi, firing in thirteen points in the first quarter. Incensed at the humiliation, Seymour triple-teamed Yardley as he inched closer to the mark. In a "fast break" made in heaven, Bird ultimately took flight and slammed home the prevailing bucket.

THE 1958–59 SEASON: FORTY MILES OF BAD ROAD

As U.S. Army private Elvis Presley was motoring around West Germany as part of the Third Armored Division, he experienced a decrease in his record sales. The Nationals, too, witnessed a slide—first in wins, down six to thirty-five, and then in attendance, falling to 107,455 seats—and they were not even playing in Europe.

Gone from the previous year were Bob Harrison, Joe Holup and Earl Lloyd, but joining the Nats roster were veteran guard George Dempsey (claimed on waivers), rookie center and first-round draft pick Connie Dierking, rookie guard and second-round draft pick Hal Greer, rookie guard and fourth-round draft pick Tommy Kearns and veteran George Yardley (traded by the Detroit Pistons for Ed Conlin). Players who were drafted but would not play included John Nacincik, Fred Grim, Jack Mimitz, Pete Tilotson and Ruel Tucker. Handling most of the court demand for Syracuse were Costello, Kerr, Schayes, Bianchi, Greer and Hopkins.

"While Nats play-by-play announcer Jim McKechnie's colorful commentary was incredibly informative and entertaining, the sights, sounds and smells of the arena were unforgettable," recalls Ross Stagnitti. "For about five dollars, you could ride the New York Central Railroad to the Erie Boulevard station, purchase a ticket at the War Memorial—to a matinee doubleheader (four NBA teams)—a program, as well as refreshments. Hearing the raucous roar of the crowd and inhaling the aroma of popcorn made a lasting impression on a wide-eyed kid from Canastota."

Opening the season with four straight home games at the Onondaga War Memorial, the team broke even in wins. It was a far different story

SYRACUSE HARDWOOD HERO

Conrad William Dierking

Position: Center - Forward
Height: 6-9
Weight: 222 lbs.
Born: October 2, 1936, in Brooklyn, New York
High School: Central in Valley Stream, New York
College: University of Cincinnati
SYR Uniform #: 8

Began career with Syracuse, 1958–59... played 135 games with the Nats...appeared in his final game with Philadelphia during the 1970–71 season..."Connie" scored over 1,000 points in three consecutive seasons for Cincinnati...selected by the Nationals in the 1958 league draft...forceful board player who compiled two seasons of over 300 personal fouls.

Connie made the move to Philadelphia with the Nats, where he was traded by the team, along with with Paul Neumann, Lee Shaffer and cash to San Francisco for Wilt Chamberlain...tough and aggressive...averaged 10.0 points and 6.7 rebounds per game during his career.

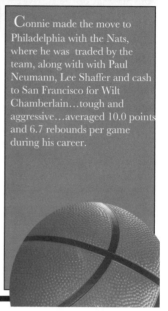

CAREER NBA	G	FG	FT	PTS
	706	2867	1360	7094

in attendance—a crowd of 3,154 viewed the home opener, less than half of last year's figure. Following four straight wins, they soon encountered eight consecutive losses that took them into the first week of December. The Nats then counterpunched with seven straight victories before seven straight losses—the inconsistency was both an irritation and a detriment.

On January 1, 1959, the Nationals sat at 14-18 and were clearly one of the most unpredictable teams in the league. The All-Star Game, played in Detroit on Friday, January 23, saw the West spank the East, 124–108, giving all but three Nats players time to think about their season; Schayes, Kerr and Costello represented their team in the Motor City. Bob Pettit of St. Louis and Elgin Baylor of Minneapolis shared the game's MVP award. Coach Seymour managed to stop the bleeding the second week of January, with five straight victories, but floundered a bit before dropping five straight the following month. The season ended, at home, with a loss to St. Louis, 132–130, to conclude at a record of 35-37, seventeen games behind Boston.

Despite the miserable winning percentage, under the .500 mark, statistically, PPG, Pythagorean and so on, the team was the second best in the league—only one team (Boston) scored more points per game and reigned superior.

The Onondaga War Memorial, the final home of the Syracuse Nationals. *Photo by author.*

The Nationals finished third in the East and beat the Knickerbockers, 2-0, in the semis. In a very tough Eastern Division Final, Syracuse lost to Boston, 4-3. (Since all home games were wins, one may wonder what would have happened had the series opened inside the War Memorial Auditorium. Syracuse was 4-5 against Minneapolis.) For all intents and purposes, *this* series was the championship, as "The Hub" swept Minneapolis four games to zero in the league finals.

Nats Notions

It took everything the Nationals had to stomach another Beantown title, exacerbated by Auerbach's victory cigars. Once having observed Knickerbockers coach Joe Lapchick smoking on the bench during a game—an activity then tolerated—Auerbach decided that when a game was within striking distance of a win, he too would light up. Boston fans enjoyed a sports tradition—"Tessie" or "Sweet Caroline"—and patiently awaited the victory signal. Although he wouldn't admit to the intimidation factor involved in the activity, opponents noticed. Boy did they; there wasn't a single member of the Syracuse bench who didn't want to grasp one of those symbols and shove it right down Arnold's throat.

The major market teams dominated the media—although nothing like it is today—shutting out the smaller teams from any recognition. That irritated an impartial Biasone, who did not share the cupidity of his fellow owners. While the losses to Boston were hard, watching the pieces fall their way may have been harder. Russell was the missing piece in the Celtics championship picture; Biasone knew it, Kerr felt it and Auerbach loved it.

Chapter 6
NATS WILT AFTER CHAMBERLAIN ARRIVES, 1959–1961

Having lost the enjoyment from NCAA basketball, Wilton Norman Chamberlain, a standout at the University of Kansas, elected to devote a year to the Harlem Globetrotters (1958–59). It would be a prudent choice, indoctrination to professional athletics; besides, the money was good, and his league of choice, the NBA, accepted only players who had completed their studies. In two seasons at the school, the Philadelphia-born seven-foot-one player averaged 29.9 points and 18.3 rebounds per game, while totaling 1,433 points and 877 rebounds; he also led Kansas to one Big Seven Championship. To say that the anticipation was high for his October 24 debut with the Philadelphia Warriors would be an understatement. Already touted by *Time*, *Life*, *Look* and *Newsweek* magazines, the event, as far as the public was concerned, couldn't come quick enough. Affectionately known as "Wilt the Stilt," "the Big Dipper" and "Chairman of the Boards," he would spend a career redefining a sport he learned to love.

THE 1959–60 SEASON: A "BIG MAN'S GAME" JUST GOT BIGGER!

When George Mikan's Minneapolis team won five league titles in six years, 1949–54, it represented the first wave of the "dominant big men"—an era when a tall center could stake a claim beneath the basket and have ascendancy over the sport. Paul Norton Seymour, himself a recipient of a surfeit of Mikan battle scars, was no stranger to what this would mean to his team's game plan. Adequate preparation and delivery could circumvent a vertical assault, a strategy that the Nationals' coach capitalized on by delivering his best year as a Syracuse mentor, posting a record of 45-30, at an impressive .600 win-loss percentage. While it would not be the highest winning percentage he would report as a league coach—that would be the following season in St. Louis—it was striking. Taking the Nationals into 279 games, Seymour had won 155 of them. His basketball skills were unquestioned, his leadership was respected and the community he loved also loved him in return.

Psychological ploys, used by coaches like Auerbach, were an attempt to gain an advantage, an edge so to speak—and they worked. They got under the skin of Syracuse players, coaches, management and even fans. But the prelude to modern-day "trash talking" could also be used as a form of retaliation. Seymour delighted in getting a rise out of Auerbach about anything, and vice versa. From the temperature in the visitors' locker room—revenge for room number seven (the visitors' locker room) at the Garden—to frivolous charges, anything could happen. Yes it was recrimination, and yes it wasn't Seymour's style, but the mental games played by the Celtics' apostle just drove him crazy. What seemed to hurt the Nats' coach the most, at least from this author's perspective, was when Auerbach denied the Celtics-Nationals rivalry—dismissing it as "small-town hype." The Celtics legend often ignored the affiliation, opting instead for the comfort provided by a New York–Boston association.

The facts, highlighted in the team's own literature (1962–63 media guide), defined the conflict. Entering the Nationals final season (1962–63), the team had an overall winning record of 467 victories and 407 defeats during the regular season. Measured against all current league franchise holders, Syracuse had more wins than every other team except one, Boston. (Boston had a winning (77-60) advantage over Syracuse.) Now that's a rivalry!

Biasone, standing at five foot six, was well aware of his league's height transition and was not opposed to it. In fact, he believed that it would lure more fans to watch his team, which it did. Attendance, albeit also attributable to Seymour's success, increased to 110,000 (sixth of eight). Countering the positive, however, was the continued league attrition. The Lakers played their final season in the Twin Cities; there wouldn't be another franchise team in Minnesota until the birth of the Timberwolves in 1989–90.

Ed Conlin, George Dempsey and Tommy Kearns departed, while the Nats added rookie guard Dick Barnett, Bradley University forward Barney

SYRACUSE HARDWOOD LEGEND

Richard Barnett

Position: Guard-Forward
Height: 6-4
Weight: 190 lbs.
Born: October 2, 1936, in Gary, Indiana
High School: Roosevelt in Gary, Indiana
College: Tennessee State University
SYR Uniform #: 5

Began career with Syracuse during the 1959–60 season…spent two seasons with the Nats…played his final game with New York during the 1973–74 season…scored over 1,000 points for ten consecutive seasons…named to the 1968 All-Star team…a durable and accurate shooter…a prolific shot artist…also with 1962–63 ABL Champions (Cleveland Pipers).

Dick was selected by Syracuse in the first round of the 1959 NBA draft…sold by the Nats to Los Angeles in September 1962…recognizable for the way he kicked both legs back as he took his jump shot…both he and his college coach John McClendon were inducted into the College Basketball Hall of Fame in 2007.

CAREER NBA	G	FG	FT	PTS
	971	6034	3290	15,358

SYRACUSE HARDWOOD HERO

Byrum William Cable

Position: Forward
Height: 6-7
Weight: 175 lbs.
Born: July 29, 1935
High School: Rochester in Rochester, PA
College: Bradley University
SYR Uniform #: 23

Began career with Detroit, 1958–59…played 125 games for the Nationals…played his final game with Baltimore during the 1963–64 season…solid rebounder and efficient shooter, "Barney" logged over 1,600 minutes with the Nats during the 1960–61 season…traded twice for Woody Sauldsberry…drafted by the Pistons in the 1958 league draft.

Barney was one of the most prolific rebounders in Bradley basketball history…third BU player to be chosen by the league draft…honored in the Greater Peoria Sports Hall of Fame…sold by the Pistons to the Nationals in November 1959…was drafted by Chicago from the Nats in the 1961 expansion draft.

CAREER NBA	G	FG	FT	PTS
	362	1012	348	2371

Cable, University of Toledo guard Jim Ray and veteran Frank Selvy (claimed on waivers). Players who were drafted but would not play included Syracuse University standout Jon Cincebox, Roger Taylor, Bob Dalton and Darnell Haney. The Nationals also drafted Bumper Tormohlen, who ended up playing with St. Louis, and Paul Neumann, who would join the team during the 1961–62 season. Schayes, Costello, Yardley, Kerr, Greer and Hopkins would handle the bulk of the hardwood minutes.

The Nats began a now seventy-five-game season at home on Saturday, October 24, against the champion Celtics. In a ruthless and high-scoring event, Syracuse succumbed to a 121–109 loss in front of 4,803 fans. Despite the engagement, the end of November found them on firm footing at 11-7, with a five-game winning streak under their belts. Having scored over the century mark in every game, until their road loss to St. Louis on November 26, it was point production at its finest.

Consistent with the previous month, the Nats, at 18-14, remained four games to the positive at the end of December. The term's stellar performance came on Sunday, December 13, as Seymour and company delivered a season high of 150 points in a decisive win (150–121) over "Wilt's Warriors."

Less than a week after the Lakers safely crash-landed their DC-3 in an Iowa cornfield, the annual All-Star gala saw the East beat the West, 125–115, in Philly (January 22). The Syracuse trio of Schayes, Costello and Yardley was part of the East contingent that witnessed rookie Wilt Chamberlain's MVP spectacle—a preview of coming attractions. The Nationals picked up some ground during the month—despite a four-game losing streak—and added to it in February, standing sound at 41-29. Combined with a 4-1 record in March, the team finished a respectable third in their division—fourteen games behind Boston. The Nationals scored over the century mark in all but three games during the regular season.

When the playoff doors opened in Philadelphia on Friday, March 11, the Nats slipped while entering. The Warriors shut down Syracuse, as the Nationals posted only ninety-two points—their worst production since Wednesday, December 9, against Minneapolis. It was a lackluster performance at best. Traveling home, they met the Warriors on Sunday and exonerated themselves with a 125–119 victory. The series, now a push at 1-1, returned to Philly for a Monday contest. The extended season—as funny as it may sound—seemed to affect the team. With the exception of Schayes, who averaged twenty-nine points and sixteen rebounds over the course of three games, Syracuse appeared tired, if not a bit lethargic. A 132–112 loss against the Warriors would finally end their annual quest; to some the team looked relieved.

In retrospect, they were an impassioned team who typically outscored their opponents; in fact, they finished second in club scoring. They also posted the highest winning percentage since the 1952–53 season. But contrasting the point production was the team's lack of defense—they gave up more than 116 PPG (sixth in the league). The semifinals loss to Philly exhibited their weakness: height—six foot nine inches just wasn't tall enough! While both Schayes and Kerr hit the boards for more than nine hundred total rebounds, Chamberlain had over twice that number.

In just fifty-seven games, Dick Barnett showed why he was the team's first-round draft pick (fourth overall) in 1959, averaging more than twelve points per game while tallying more than seven hundred points. Immediately effective, he would distinguish himself for two NBA seasons before jumping ship to play in the American Basketball League (ABL). There, with the Cleveland Pipers—owned by George Steinbrenner, the famed New York Yankees owner—Barnett would craft his trademark "Fall Back, Baby" jump shot. Kicking both his legs back during his ascent, his precision shooting led the Pipers to a 1962–63 ABL Championship. He then returned to the NBA for Los Angeles before heading to New York, where he played on two championship teams, 1969–70 and 1972–73. Receiving a doctoral degree in education from Fordham University, Barnett would later inspire many through his sports management teachings at St. Johns.

Beating St. Louis, 4-3, in the finals, "The Hub" picked up their second straight championship. Their judicious employment tactics, a piece-by-piece plan to immortality, had proven fruitful, beginning with Bob Cousy in 1950, Bill Sharman in 1951, Frank Ramsey in 1954, Jim Loscutoff in 1955 and Tom Heinsohn and Bill Russell in 1956. But "keeping up with the Joneses"—in this case, Sam Jones in 1957 and K.C. Jones in 1958—wasn't proving particularly easy for any team. When they added Gene Conley in 1958 and Tom Sanders to the Boston mix in 1960, the means appeared undeniable.

Hardwood Hyperbole

As league MVP and Rookie of the Year, a newly anointed king, Wilt Chamberlain, now had his court. While he continued to strive for new performance levels, so did Bob Cousy. The Boston impresario would top the 700 mark in assists (with 715) for the first time ever in league history; remember it was Cousy who just four years ago first topped the 600-assist mark. Picking up his second FT percentage crown, by posting an 89.3, Dolph Schayes was also as accomplished as he was accurate.

On February 5, 1960, in another sign of the apocalypse, Boston's Bill Russell became the first player to collect fifty or more rebounds in one game (yes, you read that right: one game), pulling down fifty-one while leading the Celtics to a 124–100 win over—you guessed it—Syracuse. The new single-game rebound mark broke Russell's own record of forty-nine set two seasons prior. As impressive as the Russell feat was, archrival Chamberlain was not deterred. On November 24, 1960, in a game against the Celtics—perhaps to inflict a bit of ignominy—fifty-five grabs would yield "the Big Dipper" an improved mark.

The 1960–61 Season: The Worst Winning Percentage in Team History

A leap year, at least according to the Gregorian calendar, 1960 may as well have been a leap of faith, at least in the eyes of Danny Biasone. The vehement team president stated clearly that Alex Hannum was the man he wanted. Biasone talked to no one else about filling the coaching position at Syracuse, a vacancy left by the resignation of Paul Seymour at the end of last season. As a journeyman player, Hannum's stops included Oshkosh (NBL, 1948–49), Syracuse (1949–51), Baltimore (1951–52), Rochester (1951–54), Milwaukee/St. Louis (1954–56), Fort Wayne (1956–57) and St. Louis (1956–57), an itinerant lifestyle indeed! Drafted by the Indianapolis Jets in the 1948 BAA draft, he landed in Syracuse the following year, where he averaged 7.5 PPG before being traded, along with Fred Scolari, to Baltimore for Red Rocha (1951). As a coach, Hannum was gifted, well liked and successful—his overall record, in pro and amateur ranks, including regular season and playoff competition, was 141 victories against 82 defeats, at a winning mark of .632. This was the best won-lost percentage of any coach in the league entering this new season—a point team management *never* failed to articulate.

No longer wearing a Nats uniform were Connie Dierking, Bob Hopkins, Togo Palazzi, Jim Ray, Frank Selvy, Paul Seymour and George Yardley. The team welcomed to their roster veteran guard Ernie Beck (sold by the Hawks), forward Dave Gambee (sold by the Hawks), center Swede Halbrook and forward Cal Ramsey (sold by the Knickerbockers). Players who were drafted but would not play included Wilbur Trosch, Carl Cole, Jim Mudd, Bernie Kauffman, LeMoyne College standout Dick Lynch and Bernie Findlay. Lee

SYRACUSE HARDWOOD HERO

David P. Gambee

Position: Forward
Height: 6-7
Weight: 215 lbs.
Born: April 16, 1937, in Portland, Oregon
High School: Corvallis in Corvallis, Oregon
College: Oregon State University
SYR Uniform #: 20

Began career with St. Louis, 1958–59...spent three seasons with Nats...played his final game with San Francisco during the 1969–70 season...tough, quick and forceful, "Dave" was outstanding from the charity stripe...always played aggressive against former clubs...scored over 1,000 points during a season four times...sold by St. Louis to Syracuse in 1960.

Dave followed the Nats to Philadelphia before being drafted by San Diego...also spent time with the Bucks, Pistons and Warriors...member of 1967 Philly championship team...played alongside Bobby Plump (Jimmy Chitwood in the movie *Hoosiers*) in the annual 1958 East-West All-Star Game in New York City...Pac-10 HOF.

CAREER NBA	G	FG	FT	PTS
	750	2820	2295	7935

Shaffer was the Nats' first-round pick and would join the team during the 1961–62 season, as would third-round pick (twenty-first overall), forward Joe Roberts. Herschell Turner, the team's sixth-round pick, would later surface in the American Basketball Association (ABA). Hannum would rely on Schayes (F-C), Greer (G-F), Kerr (C-F), Costello (G), Gambee (F) and Barnett (G-F) to carry the weight.

Perhaps the most intriguing of the new additions was Harvey Wade "Swede" Halbrook, born on January 30, 1933. At seven foot three, he was the tallest player in the college ranks. A product of Oregon State University, he landed in Syracuse through the 1956 draft and stayed for two seasons. During his brief career, all spent with the Nationals, he played 143 games at 5.5 PPG. For fans, his size made him an attraction; people would flock to him for autographs or a snapshot. The attention was a bit disconcerting to the introverted Halbrook, however, who preferred the solitude of a hotel room and the skills of knitting. To his coach, Halbrook was an enigma; he would just disappear, for days at a time, leaving team personnel concerned for his safety. More than once, Hannum had no other choice but to have the Syracuse police put out an APB for his giant. Often, Swede would just casually reappear, unaware of the ruckus he had caused and never explaining where he had been.

The home opener, against Philadelphia on Saturday, October 22, reintroduced Hannum, or the "Bald Eagle" as he was affectionately known, to Syracuse and the rest of Central New York. But despite the coach's warm welcome—from 4,677 fans—and trademark smile, the first of three losses in a row would prove little more than a prelude to disaster. His team was inconsistent right from the start: three losses, a win, three more losses, three wins, four more losses…you get the picture. The departure of three frontcourt veterans was an Achilles heel, and one that Hannum could not immediately correct—his youngsters needed more playing time.

When January concluded, they were 24-27 and in need of a defensive rededication—summoned by Hannum, the request was accepted. The team improved the following month, posting a five-game winning streak that would take them to 36-33. But March would prove to be an absolute disaster, as the Nats could only claim a pair of victories. A finish below .500, at 38-41, marked the end of the regular season—.481, the worst winning percentage Alex Hannum had ever posted as an NBA coach.

From an exposure perspective, the Nationals did manage to take their show on the road locally for four games in 1961: in Utica, against Cincinnati, on January 2; against Los Angeles, on Sunday, January 22; in Rochester, on Sunday, January 7, against the Knickerbockers; and on Saturday, February 18, against the Warriors. The rush and slush of a Central New York winter can intimidate even a local traveler.

Cynicism often infiltrates professional sports, as it did this season when the Nationals made the playoffs for an unprecedented fifteenth successive season—opening on Tuesday, March 14, in Philadelphia. Syracuse felt they had nothing to lose—and truly didn't. They took three straight against the Warriors, averaging 112 points. It would, despite a trio of victories, be a much different story when they moved northeast to Boston. On Sunday, March 19, the Nats dropped their first game against Boston, 128–115, and then won at home on Tuesday, 115–98, before losing the next three.

Paradoxically, the most productive team in the league—averaging 121.3 PPG—finished third in their division. Six players scored more than one thousand points (Schayes, Greer, Barnett, Gambee, Costello and Kerr), and while attendance was up from the previous season, it was still the worst in the league at 112,394. It was a mercurial position, the Nationals' nadir.

Durable and resilient, Dave Gambee had an accurate eye from the charity stripe and immediately made a contribution by averaging 13.7 PPG. The real-life link between the movie *Hoosiers*, the story of the 1954 Indiana state champions, Milan High School and the Syracuse Nationals, Gambee played alongside Bobby Plump (Jimmy Chitwood in the movie) in the annual 1958 East-West All-Star Game in New York City. He was a welcome Syracuse addition.

Having shellacked St. Louis, four games to one, in the finals, Boston polished their third straight crown—one for each leaf of the clover-like plant.

Never before had the league witnessed such productivity and efficiency during a season. Statistical leadership focused on one man, Wilt Chamberlain, whose point production and statistics were undeniable: 3,033 points, the first year above the 3,000 mark; 2,149 rebounds, the first season above the 2,000 plateau; and a 50.9 field goal efficiency, the first season above 50 percent. It was success at thirty-five inches or less!

THE 1961 NBA ALL-STAR GAME

A decade earlier, Haskell Cohen joined the league office. College basketball had been suffering from point-shaving scandals, giving the professional stage the perfect opportunity to attract new fans. Cohen and Commissioner Maurice Podoloff—the league's dynamic duo—met with Boston owner Walter A. Brown for an idea session, a league "think tank" if you will. It was there that Cohen suggested an All-Star Game—it wasn't a novel idea, it just made sense (or *cents*). Other sports, such as baseball, were holding elite extravaganzas; why not professional basketball? Brown agreed and put the then modest affair inside—where else?—the Boston Garden, on March 2, 1951. (It was also Cohen who would attend an exhibition game inside a Syracuse gym in August 1954, at which a 24-second clock was being examined; he would act as Biasone's time keeper.) The gala event took over a decade to reach the Salt City, but it did make it here.

It was, without a doubt, the greatest assembly of hardwood talent ever to appear in the city of Syracuse, and they were here to play a basketball game. It was so impressive that when panelists were asked to select the fifty greatest players in NBA history (1996), without regard to position, ten of them had attended *this* All-Star Game (Oscar Robertson, Bob Pettit, Elgin Baylor, Jerry West, Wilt Chamberlain, Bob Cousy, Dolph Schayes, Bill Russell, Hal Greer and Paul Arizin)—20 percent of the greatest athletes to ever play a particular sport did so under one roof in Central New York.

On Tuesday, January 17, 1961, the Syracuse Nationals presented the eleventh annual All-Star Game on their home court inside the War Memorial. The Nats had just returned from a northeastern swing of neutral courts, having played the Celtics in Philadelphia on Thursday, January 12, followed by the Knickerbockers in Boston on Friday, before returning home. Spirits were high—or as high as one may expect from a 19-24 record—as the team had defeated the Warriors, 116–113, on Sunday.

To host an All-Star Game in any major professional sport is a thrill for any city, and Syracuse was no different. The excitement could be felt just walking down Salina Street, as you could overhear conversations about Chamberlain, Russell and, of course, Paul Seymour, who was returning home to coach the West squad.

The Syracuse Junior Chamber of Commerce hosted the All-Star Luncheon at the Hotel Syracuse. A Syracuse landmark since 1924, the historic building is located conveniently in the heart of downtown (500 South Warren Street). Fans flocked to the hotel's beautiful lobby looking for an opportunity to see one of their hardwood heroes in person. The second-floor lobby was the perfect perch for stargazing, as most players entered through one of two entrances, adorned by marble staircases with brass railings, that led to the check-in area. Two-story octagonal columns are scattered across the lobby, reinforcing a coffered ceiling enhanced by elaborate chandeliers. Even the tallest and best league stars looked small by comparison.

Fans braving the winter air delighted viewing the War Memorial marquee that announced the game ("THE 11TH ANNUAL N.B.A. ALL-STAR GAME, TUESDAY") in large red block letters before entering the facility. If the cold air didn't send shivers down your spine, the sign certainly would. Once inside, many picked up a copy of the red, white and blue souvenir program, a value at fifty cents, before entering through the turnstiles into the hallway and through the main doors leading courtside.

A well-dressed crowd of 8,016 filled the arena, many keeping their coats on for additional warmth. The War Memorial seemed perfect that night, decked out to perfection; Syracuse was indeed a proud host.

Dressed in blue uniforms, the West was coached by the familiar face of Hawks coach Paul Seymour. Respected and beloved, he was given a hometown welcome. The West would start Oscar Robertson (Cincinnati), Elgin Baylor (Los Angeles), Gene Shue (Detroit) and two of his own in Bob Pettit (St. Louis) and Clyde Lovellette (St. Louis). The bench would include Jerry West (Los Angeles), Walter Dukes (Detroit), Bailey Howell (Detroit), Hot Rod Hundley (Los Angeles), Cliff Hagen (St. Louis) and Wayne Embry (Cincinnati).

The East, wearing white, had Red Auerbach at the helm. Wilt Chamberlain (Philadelphia), Richie Guerin (New York), local hero Dolph Schayes (Syracuse) and two Celtics, Bob Cousy and Tom Heinsohn, would start.

Auerbach's reserves were Bill Russell (Boston), Tom Gola (Philadelphia), Hall Greer (Syracuse), Paul Arizin (Philadelphia), Willie Naulls (New York) and Larry Costello (Syracuse). Worth noting is that only Cousy and Schayes had participated in all eleven of the annual events.

The opening tip favored the West, who guided Clyde Lovellette into position—about five feet above the key—for his classic one-handed set shot. Swoosh! The first basket of the annual gala set an extraordinary pace. The East then tried to work the ball inside to Chamberlain, who turned from a low-key pivot position to miss the mark with his fadeaway jumper. After some missed tap-ins, Pettit controlled the carom and released a deep pass to Lovellette for an easy layup. The master playmaker, Bob Cousy then took command of the East and charged the key. An over-the-shoulder pass—common for this era—to Schayes driving the lane was executed masterfully for the first East score. What some consider "flash" by Cousy, he deems as efficiency; he is that gifted. Bob Pettit then converted a careless pass into the next score for the West. Another West player, this time Jerry West, coerced a steal and fed Lovellette again atop the key for a bucket; the West raced away to a 28–9 advantage. Such is the opening action of the first quarter that ended with the West up 47–19.

The second quarter began as the East took the tip and an eventual Gola score. Running a classic weave above the key, the East hoped to open a charging lane. Russell then began his rebound quest in haste and in arrears. Effective from the outside, Lovellette, along with Robertson, provided the Western assault. Off the bench, Willie Naulls was also impressive, with his lethal outside jump shot for the East. The West, now with a comfortable margin, began a top-of-the-key weave to slow the pace a bit and revivify their attack force. A Cousy behind-the-back pass to Greer exhilarated the crowd and was perhaps the most exciting play of the quarter. Tom Heinsohn took the final shot of the half with a sharp successful jumper from above the arch. At the half, the West remained dominant, 84–62.

The capacity crowd was then treated to a halftime show, center-court, by the trickery of the Dover Ohio Basketeers, six youngsters ages twelve to fourteen who performed ball-handling similar in style to the Harlem Globetrotters. It was a welcome diversion to the blistering pace being set by the evening's feature. "I bought two tickets for the All-Star Game," recalls Bill Martin, "and gave one to my father for Christmas. We attended the game together." To Martin, as well as other area residents, hardwood dreams were an adjunct to Central New York living.

Wilt controlled the second-half tip to Baylor and over to Shue, and the West was set in motion. The "Cousy-Russell" twosome began their all-too-

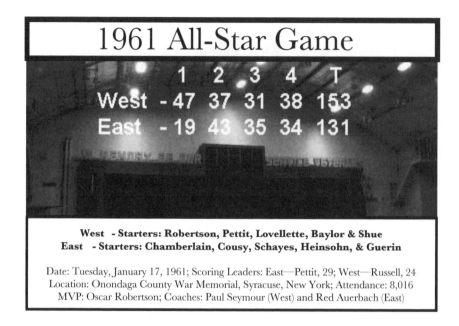

1961 All-Star Game

	1	2	3	4	T
West -	47	37	31	38	153
East -	19	43	35	34	131

West - Starters: Robertson, Pettit, Lovellette, Baylor & Shue
East - Starters: Chamberlain, Cousy, Schayes, Heinsohn, & Guerin

Date: Tuesday, January 17, 1961; Scoring Leaders: East—Pettit, 29; West—Russell, 24
Location: Onondaga County War Memorial, Syracuse, New York; Attendance: 8,016
MVP: Oscar Robertson; Coaches: Paul Seymour (West) and Red Auerbach (East)

familiar attack plan that reached a crescendo with a convincing slam. Cousy, a master of screen artistry, placed the block above the key, opening Gola for an easy bucket. Witnessing Chamberlain retrieve a Robertson shot out of the stratosphere ignited onlookers. Hot Rod Hundley, no stranger to any audience, remained deadly for the West with his precision hook. At 115–97, in favor of the West, the quarter ended.

Fatigue was now becoming evident on the faces of the starters as the fourth quarter got underway. Russell remained relentless under the boards, on his way to eleven rebounds for the East. Fans continued in their delight with Cousy's ball handling in a command performance. The teams, averaging six points per minute, continued to knock down more than a decade's worth of records. When the buzzer sounded, it was 153–131, with the West victorious.

The Royals' Oscar Robertson, arguably the most complete player to play the game of basketball, took All-Star MVP honors. For the West, Pettit (twenty-nine), Robertson (twenty-three) and Lovellette (twenty-one) all scored above the twenty-point mark, while the East was led by both Russell (twenty-four) and Schayes (twenty-one). A satisfied crowd bundled themselves up to fight the elements of an icy New York evening. One last glimpse at the War Memorial marquee is all that that they needed to verify that they had just witnessed basketball history.

Chapter 7
THE SIXTIES,
1961–1963

I t was an achievement unthinkable by most, a paragon of proficiency. Setting the single-game scoring record, by tallying 100 points in a 169–147 victory over New York, Wilt Chamberlain of the Warriors became immortal on March 2, 1962. It was hardwood majesty so prolific that the term "dominance" was redefined. Chamberlain, already a prodigious league force, was slowly becoming a paradigm in all of sports, intimidated by no man and no issue.

The phenomenon originated from Hershey, Pennsylvania, where the Warriors strategically added "home" games to enhance their fan base. Far from being afraid of the no. 13 (his jersey), Chamberlain could not be deterred, either by Darrall Imhoff and Cleveland Buckner—both substitutes for regular ailing center Phil Jordon—or by anyone. With forty-one points by halftime (twenty-three in the first quarter), Philadelphia's native son then tallied twenty-eight in the third quarter on his way to the magic mark. Perceiving the inevitable, along with a bit of history, Hershey fans began shouting "Give it to Wilt! Give it to Wilt!" The Philly players obliged, feeding Chamberlain like a hungry lion. The Knickerbockers tried fruitlessly to foul alternative combatants, but nothing could counter the Chamberlain offensive. The Warriors, exemplary of their moniker and in support of their teammate, retaliated through return fire—in the form of aggressive fouling.

With forty-six seconds left, a short shot—initiated by a feed from forward Joe Ruklick—dropped, and the damage was done. Spectators spilled out into the court, as Chamberlain beamed. He then headed to the locker room, where PR man Harvey Pollack, doing his best Irving Rudd imitation, penned

"100" on a piece of paper and handed it to the conqueror. The press shot like infantry during the Normandy landings of World War II. At this hour, Goliath had no detractors.

The numbers spoke volumes: thirty-six for sixty-three from the field and twenty-eight for thirty-two from the foul line, a remarkable feat for a man whose career free throw percentage was an abysmal .511; he also broke his previous NBA scoring record of seventy-eight points set less than three months earlier. If this were not evidence enough that the game was in transition, there was more. The only occurrence of a player averaging a triple-double throughout a season also transpired, as Oscar Robertson averaged 30.8 points, 11.4 assists and 12.5 rebounds per game. Perhaps we needed to be reminded that productivity is never a mishap but instead a result of quality, desire and its strategic implementation.

THE 1961–62 SEASON: AFTER 706 GAMES, SCHAYES SITS

For the third consecutive season, the league schedule was expanded, adding a game to reach eighty. Prolonged seasons do not bode well for any league player whose typical shelf-life is under a decade. (Today, the figure most quoted is five years.) League dynamics, which often means survival contrasted against profit, will continue during the organization's maturity. While one game doesn't seem like much, tell that to the veterans—a decade earlier, the team schedule stood at sixty-six.

Baseball's Roger Maris, of the New York Yankees, and his pursuit of the single-season home run record, dominated newspaper sports sections for weeks, leaving little room for hardwood notes. Roster changes for the Nats included the departure of Dick Barnett, Ernie Beck, Barney Cable and Cal Ramsey and the addition of veteran Joe Graboski (sold by Chicago), rookie guard Paul Neumann and rookie forward Lee Shaffer. The Nats also drafted Ben Warley, who would join the team during the 1962–63 season; Chuck Osborne, who would only play four games during the year; and Hank Whitney, who would later surface in the ABA. Players drafted but who did not play included Chris Smith, Don Jacobson, Billy Joe Price, Roger Newman, Dave Mills, Rex Tippitt, Syracuse star Pete Chudy and LeMoyne standout Dick Sammons. The team, soon hampered by impairments, relied on Red Kerr (C-F), Hal Greer (G-F), Dave Gambee (F), Al Bianchi (G), Larry Costello (G) and Joe Roberts (F) to carry most of the production load.

SYRACUSE HARDWOOD HERO

Paul R. Neumann

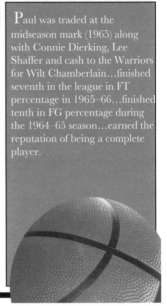

Position: Guard
Height: 6-1
Weight: 175 lbs.
Born: January 30, 1938
High School: Newport Harbor in Newport Harbor, CA
College: Stanford University
SYR Uniform #: 5

Began career with the Nationals, 1961–62…played his final game with San Francisco during the 1966–67 season…a durable playmaker…selected by Syracuse in the fourth round (twenty-seventh pick) of the 1959 league draft…replaced both Costello and Greer when they were injured (1961–62) …entered the league as fifth-highest scorer in Stanford history.

Paul was traded at the midseason mark (1965) along with Connie Dierking, Lee Shaffer and cash to the Warriors for Wilt Chamberlain…finished seventh in the league in FT percentage in 1965–66…finished tenth in FG percentage during the 1964–65 season…earned the reputation of being a complete player.

CAREER NBA	G	FG	FT	PTS
	453	1827	1335	4989

The Packers, who had entered the league as a major market expansion team, opened the Nats season in Syracuse on Saturday, October 21. A modest crowd of 3,665—down by more than 1,000 from the previous year—watched as Coach Hannum and his team trounced Chicago by twenty points, 123–103. But the team was unpredictable right from the start, never compiling more than a couple wins in a row; the end of November found them 9-10. Even worse was December, as the team encountered two losing streaks: the first in five games and the second in four, leaving them 14-22 at year's end. Injuries, never an easy dilemma for a coach, were the basis for the decline.

A new year meant the logical "new beginning speech," a bit of Coaching 101, Hannum concurred. Vigilance was reestablished, and for a while Syracuse prevailed. The Nats went on a seven-game winning streak, January 6–18, which included a nice victory over Boston, 127–117, in Rochester on January 13. Three days later, the league held its All-Star Game in St. Louis, Missouri, with the West hammering the East 150–130. The Syracuse contribution included Hal Greer, Dolph Schayes and an injured Larry Costello. Local favorite Bob Pettit, with a brilliant rebounding performance, picked up the game's MVP award. The annual break appeared to be a distraction for the team, as their "winning ways" concluded at the Boston Garden on Friday, January 19—Syracuse was soundly defeated by the champions, 128–103. The team then lost their next five games and stood 25-30 at the end of the month.

Syracuse destroyed St. Louis, 135–101, in Utica, to open the month of February (on the second). The victory was a prelude to a stretch that brought the Nats back to an even .500 (36-36) mark entering March. The club would finish solid, winning 5 of 8, to take their record to a respectable 41-39. It was an impressive finish considering that Hannum only had seven players available during the last few weeks.

The Nationals, back in the playoffs, kept their postseason streak alive. It was Philadelphia against Syracuse for the best of five in the East Semis. The Nationals lost two, won two and then lost the final game in Philly, 121–104. It was another third-place finish, nineteen games behind the Celtics. The year ended with Boston winning their fourth straight crown, beating Los Angeles, four games to three.

It was a peculiar year for the Nationals. Even though they outscored their opponents, and played games in both Utica and Rochester, they failed to dramatically increase their fan base—and it was evident. While four members of the team scored more than one thousand points (Greer, Gambee, Kerr and Shaffer), noticeably absent was a familiar face. Hampered by injuries, Dolph Schayes—the finest player ever to wear any Syracuse basketball uniform—convalesced, putting an end to a streak of 706 consecutive games played. Injury also befell his teammates Hal Greer, Joe Graboski and Swede Halbrook.

LEAGUE NOTES

Statistical records continued to wither, as Chamberlain destroyed two key thresholds: points (4,029), the first season over the 4,000-point point; and rebounds (2,052), the first player to ever record more than 2,000 grabs. Along with Oscar Robertson and his assists (899), the first season over the 800 mark, no record was safe. But even a new generation had trouble combating the inevitable, as veteran Schayes picked up his third and final FT percentage crown with a mark of 89.9.

The Most Valuable Player award went to Bill Russell of Boston, and the Rookie of the Year recipient was Walt Bellamy of Chicago. Despite the record-melting year, this was the last season of the league on the NBC network. A staple from 1955 until 1962, the weekly presentation of the National Broadcasting Corporation would no longer bring Dr. Naismith's game into our living rooms.

THE 1962–63 SEASON: A TACIT DEPARTURE

When the phone rang, Danny Biasone picked it up and received confirmation that the Warriors were looking westward to San Francisco. An essential part of the league's foundation and a fixture for decades in Philadelphia, the Warriors, whose lineage in basketball dated back to the Sphas of the 1920s, had been a major market stronghold. Once again, that feeling in the pit of his stomach returned, as questions of stability chaperoned the emotion. A West Coast team meant increased travel costs and time—the issues weren't unexpected, but the reality might have been. Countering his concern were the circumstances: Philadelphia was a popular basketball market and a fantastic venue for all sports. Certainly, he thought, they would not be denied their pastime.

Central New York Basketball, Incorporated, had some assistance bringing them into a new decade, including Jack Egan, chairman of the board; Ed Peterson, first vice-president; Ralph S. Crear, second vice-president; W. Carrol Coyne, third vice-president; John H. Pirro, secretary; and Berard W. Sarno, treasurer. Also included were Directors Donald Cain, William V. Haggerty, Sanford Harrison, Ernie Maffaei, Dan O'Brien, Dr. Max Rifken, Charles Schoeneck and Oscar Swanson. Additional resources were provided by Gerald Salisbury, Red Parton, Leon Dumas, Mike Dempsey, John Testone and Ed Youmans. It would be the eventual rendition of a proud supporting staff.

Around the league, other issues were transpiring: the Cincinnati Royals were promptly shifted to the league's East Division as a replacement for the Warriors; the Packers were renamed the Zephyrs (a Chicago identity crisis perhaps); another television network, ABC—a rival to NBC—began televising league games, which it would do until the 1973–74 season; and the American Basketball League became a factor as Globetrotters' owner and legend Abe Saperstein—in retaliation for not being given a league franchise—began his own organization.

Coach Hannum had a fine rookie crop greet him in the fall. Roster changes saw the departure of Joe Graboski, Swede Halbrook and Chuck Osborne, while the Nats added forward and first-round draft pick Len Chappell, third-

SYRACUSE HARDWOOD HERO

Leonard R. Chappell

Position: Forward - Center
Height: 6-8
Weight: 240 lbs.
Born: January 31, 1941, in Portage, Pennsylvania
High School: Portage in Portage, PA
College: Wake Forest University
SYR Uniform #: 23

Began career with the Nationals, 1962–63...sought by Coach Hannum for his aggressive play...played his final game with the Dallas Chaparrals, of the ABA, during the 1971–72 season...durable and accurate, "Len" was a 1964 league All-Star...admired for his humble and sincere demeanor...he was sold by Philadelphia to the Knickerbockers in 1963.

Len was named ACC Men's Basketball Player of the Year in 1961 and 1962...was the ACC tournament's all-time leading scorer until Duke University's J.J. Redick surpassed him in 2006...named as one of the fifty greatest players in Atlantic Coast Conference history in 2002...a fan favorite.

CAREER NBA	G	FG	FT	PTS
	591	2212	1197	5621

SYRACUSE HARDWOOD LEGEND

Chester Walker

Position: Forward - Guard
Height: 6-6
Weight: 212 lbs.
Born: February 22, 1940, in Benton Harbor, Michigan
High School: Benton Harbor in Benton Harbor, Michigan
College: Bradley University
SYR Uniform #: 25

Began career with the Nationals, 1962–63...payed his final game with the Bulls during the 1974–75 season...durable and accurate, "Chet the Jet" was a seven-time All-Star...scored over 1,000 points for twelve consecutive seasons...led the league in FT percentage during 1970–71 season...a spectacular offensive player.

Chet was selected by the Nats in the second round (fourteenth pick) of the 1962 draft...named to the league's first All-Rookie Team in 1963...played his final six seasons with Chicago and never averaged less than 19.2 PPG...a starting forward on the 1966–67 Philadelphia team, perhaps the best team of all time.

CAREER NBA	G	FG	FT	PTS
	1032	6876	5079	18,831

Syracuse, NY—1955: Dolph Schayes of the Syracuse Nationals attempts a hook shot against the Philadelphia 76ers in 1955 in Syracuse, New York. Copyright 1955 NBAE. *Photo by NBA Photo Library/NBAE via Getty Images.*

round draft pick guard Porter Meriwether and rookie forwards Chet Walker (second-round draft selection) and Ben Warley. Players who were drafted but did not play included St. Bonaventure standout Bob McCully, Larry Van Eman, Bob Sharpenter and Vince Brewer; John Windsor, who would end up playing for San Francisco, was also selected by the Nats. Handling floor production, Hannum would rely on Greer, Kerr, Shaffer, Costello, Walker and Neumann.

What would be the final season for the Nationals opened up against Los Angeles on Saturday night, October 20, at 8:00 p.m. A noticeably sharper Syracuse team took the initial victory, 108–102, and soon added two others; by the end of November, the team stood comfortably at 13-6. December was much the same, highlighted by a nice Saturday night (December 8) home

SYRACUSE NATIONALS—THE FINAL TEAM

1962-63: THE PLAYERS

Hal Greer **; 1562 - PTS; 2631 - MP; 600 - FG;
   362 - FT ; 19.5 PPG
Lee Shaffer ** Led team in production per minute.
Red Kerr ** .474 FG%; 1039 - TRB;
Chet Walker (R)
Larry Costello; .881 FT%; 334 - A;
Len Chappell (R) **
Dave Gambee
Paul Neumann **
Dolph Schayes
Al Bianchi
Joe Roberts
Ben Warley (R)
Porter Meriwether (R)

COACH: ALEX HANNUM

*Ranked by PTS; ** Played in all 80 games. (R) - Rookie;
Bold = All-Star; Attendance: 161, 593.

* Source: Team Records.

Coach Hannum finished second in the Eastern Division…lost Eastern Division Semifinals to Cincinnati (3-2)….season record 48-32…had a nine-game winning streak (2/24/63–3/12/63)….a team designed for point production— first in league at 121.6 PPG…scored 163 points in win over San Francisco (3/10/63)…played three games in Rochester and one game in Utica, New York…finished regular season with three straight losses…Shaffer led team in playoff production at 136 PTS…scored over 115 points in all five playoff games (2-3).

1962-63 SEASON	G	FG	FT	PTS
	80	3690	2350	9730

victory over Boston, 102–97. When the year drew to a close, Syracuse stood a resolved 19-15.

Adding a decisive 120–95 victory over St. Louis ignited the new calendar year, and by All-Star break the team was five games to the positive. In Los Angeles, on January 16, the East beat the West, 115–108, in the midseason classic. The Syracuse contingent included Johnny Kerr, Lee Shaffer and Hal Greer. Boston's Bill Russell picked up the game's MVP award.

A savory home victory over archrival Boston, 149–148, on January 19 began the second half of the season as the team marched steadily forward. In February, the squad assembled a solid five-game winning streak before entering March like a lion during a nine-game winning streak (including a record 163–148 home win).

The cessation to the regular season home schedule came on a Saturday evening, March 16. It was an 8:00 p.m. appointment with a group of antagonists from Boston, and while victory would have tasted so sweet, it was not to be had, as a 125–121 loss befell our boys. The last regular season game, one day later, was also a loss to the same team, only in the Garden, 125–116. A record of 48-32, second in the East, would close the book.

Facing Cincinnati in the East Semis would be no easy task for Syracuse. Taking two wins at home, and two losses on the road, the Nationals found themselves at home on Tuesday, March 26. In a dauntless effort by both contenders, the Royals shocked Syracuse with an overtime victory 131–127, to win game five and the series. Delivering their fifth straight championship, Boston, who had defeated the Royals, then beat Los Angeles, four games to two, in the finals.

Larry Costello took over where Dolph left off, leading the league in free throw percentage with a mark of .881. The MVP award went to Bill Russell of Boston, and the Rookie of the Year recipient was Terry Dischinger of Chicago.

Syracuse had outscored all their opponents, and mathematically, if statistics drove accountability, the team was outstanding. An apportioned attack saw Greer, Shaffer and Kerr each score more than one thousand points, and all but three team players exceed the five-hundred-point plateau. The formidable and accurate Red Kerr, a board veteran at age thirty, grabbed more than one thousand caroms and led the team in outside accuracy. Playmaker Larry Costello guided Syracuse with 334 assists. Attendance improved, from 112,000 to well over 161,000, as the final curtain dropped.

Coaching Records

Coach	1st Season	#S	W	L	P-W	P-L
Benny Borgmann	1946–47	2	45	59	1	6
Al Cervi	1948–49	9	334	224	35	29
Paul Seymour	1956–57	4	155	124	9	11
Alex Hannum	1960–61	3	127	112	8	10

Notes: #S—*includes partial season;*
P—*playoffs; seventeen seasons, in two*
leagues, at a regular season record of
661-519. Playoffs record 53-56.

Individual Records—One Season

TP (Total Points)	1,868	Dolph Schayes	1960–61
PPG (Points Per Game)	24.9	Dolph Schayes	1957–58
FGA (Field Goal Att.)	1,595	Dolph Schayes	1960–61
FG (Field Goals)	644	Hal Greer	1961–62
FG% (Field Goal Per.)	.482	Larry Costello	1960–61
FTA (Free Throw Att.)	783	Dolph Schayes	1960–61
FT (Free Throws)	680	Dolph Schayes	1960–61
FT% (Free Throw Per.)	.9045	Dolph Schayes	1956–57
TRB (Total Rebounds)	1,176	Johnny Kerr	1961–62
AST (Assists)	483	Paul Seymour	1954–55
Consecutive FT	50	Dolph Schayes	1957–58

Source: Team Records; Att.—attempts

REFLECTION

Staring through a chain link fence at remnants of a foundation that once represented more than 2912 James Street, I couldn't help but feel moved. Basketball always promised us that we wouldn't have to grow up, I thought, and the Eastwood Sports Center was part of that promise. To think that one man's vision—an Italian immigrant who chose Syracuse as his home and a check for $5,000, a worthy sum in 1946—established a seasoned participant in one of the four major professional sports was beyond my comprehension. Accomplished during the infancy of a sport—perhaps the most challenging time—and in a city that was not a metropolis, the organization not only persisted through overwhelming obstacles but prospered as well. They were playoff staples, even league champions! This team put smiles on faces, names in record books and our heroes in Springfield, all while looking into the eyes of their Eastwood neighbors and believing that dreams really do come true.

THE NATs

Arenas
Syracuse Armory Building, 1946–48
State Fair Coliseum, 1948–51
Onondaga County War Memorial, 1951–63

Team History	W	L	PCT
(Prior to '46) Independent	-	-	-
(1946–49) NBL (167)	85	82	.509
(1949–63) NBA (1,013)	576	437	.569

Team Colors
Varied: blue and gold; red, white and blue
Division Championships (3)
1949–50, 1951–52, 1954–55
Finals Appearances (3)
1949–50, 1953–54, 1954–55
League Championships (1)
1954–55

The sidewalks in front of where the Eastwood Sports Center once stood. *Photo by author.*

Chapter 8

A COGNITIVE TRANSITION

It had been more than a year—about Thanksgiving of last year—since the Syracuse Nationals took two key games from the Celtics to vault into first place. The Nats were back, "on the top rung," the newspapers sung, although most fans were hard pressed to remember precisely when that was and how long they had been there. (Even *Sports Illustrated* praised their newfound glory, December 3, 1962.) It was almost a year since we last saw the familiar figure of Danny Biasone, standing resolute alongside coach Hannum, directing traffic like a Crouse-Hinds stoplight, a year since we saw Mayor William Walsh and the city hall contingent settling municipal problems between court occupations—there was no possession arrow back then; the gesticulations spoke for themselves! It had been just about a year since we last saw the best backcourt impresarios the Nats had had in years, Hal Greer and Larry Costello, the pair masterfully conducting able accompaniment. It had been about a year since we saw a stately Dolph Schayes, a reflection of what he was—which was still better than most—trotting down the court in that distinctive style he had, raising his fist in another sign of court supremacy. It had been about a year—a term without a team, one that passed too fast.

A group of teenagers entered the War Memorial looking for Billy Backus fight tickets. Backus, a promising welterweight and the nephew of boxing legend Carmen Basilio, was three years old when Biasone brought professional basketball to Syracuse. The Nationals would win their only league championship exactly two months before Basilio would win his first world title. On this day, the Nats were no longer on the court, and Basilio was no longer in the ring.

Nats Home Team Advantage
Onondaga County War Memorial

50 Personal Fouls	v. New York, February 15, 1953
43 Assists	v. Philadelphia, February 27, 1955
.962, FT percentage	v. Minneapolis, November 9, 1958
67 Field Goals	v. Boston, March 3, 1960
163, Highest Point Total	v. San Francisco, March 10, 1963
86, Highest First Half Total	v. Detroit, February 12, 1961
86, Highest Second Half Total	v. Philadelphia, February 21, 1962

Selected team performances.

THE PHILADELPHIA TRANSITION

One year after the Warriors left for San Francisco, the Syracuse Nationals were purchased—the amount often given is $500,000—by paper magnate Irv Kosloff and Ike Richman. The team had lost over $39,000 the previous season. That was in the spring of 1963, with league approval for franchise shift occurring on May 22. Returning professional basketball to Philadelphia also meant an appropriate moniker, which the city found with the name 76ers (August 6).

1963–64...1966–67

Separating Philadelphia from a championship would be four challenging seasons, but it would be far from a simple task. Player-coach Dolph Schayes would accept the responsibility for the first thirty-six months of the tetralogy, followed by Alex Hannum, who would deliver the team down the stretch. The former yielded two third-place finishes in the division, followed by an Eastern title. In 240 games, he won 129, lost 111 and posted his highest annual winning percentage as a coach, .688. That occurred in his final

Road Show—Point Production

Dolph Schayes   50 points v. Boston, February 1, 1959
Hal Greer   45 points v. Boston, February 14, 1959
Johnny Kerr   42 points v. Cincinnati, December 20, 1957
Dave Gambee   36 points v. NY in Utica, February 24, 1962
Lee Shaffer   34 points v. LA in Rochester, December 16, 1961
Larry Costello   33 points v. Philadelphia, January 5, 1958
Al Bianchi   27 points v. Minneapolis, December 11, 1958
Swede Halbrook   19 points v. Philadelphia, January 18, 1961
Joe Roberts   19 points v. LA in Philly, December 27, 1961

Selected individual performances on the road.

Philadelphia in Syracuse

Post-Nationals Visits

1963–64	January 8 and 18, 1964; March 3, 1964*
1964–65	December 13, 1964; January 6 and 23, 1965; February 6 and 28, 1965*
1965–66	December 11, 1965; January 6, 1966; February 12, 1966*
1966–67	December 17, 1966; February 28, 1967**
1967–68	December 30, 1967**
1968–69	December 8, 1968; January 30, 1969; February 27, 1969***
1969–70	December 28, 1969; February 19, 1970***

* Dolph Schayes, Coach
** Alex Hannum, Coach
*** Jack Ramsay, Coach

season—also a term for which he was named Coach of the Year. Schayes would bid adieu to the City of Brotherly Love in stark contrast to the moniker. (Perhaps love had a height limit.) At season's end, he was replaced as coach by Alex Hannum.

During a decade often defined by turbulence, catharsis found its way courtside when San Francisco traded Wilt Chamberlain to Philadelphia on January 15, 1965, for Connie Dierking, Paul Neumann, Lee Shaffer and cash. One of the reasons why Wilt Chamberlain was reluctant to return to Philadelphia was Dolph Schayes. It was an intense environment, complicated by overwhelming issues, factors beyond the control of both great players. (Chamberlain, who put the "I" in narcissism, would also author the coaching headstones of Hannum, Neil Johnston, Frank McGuire and Butch van Breda Kolff.)

A former Nationals player and a league coach since the 1956–57 season, Hannum was the last man to take a winner past Boston (the 1957–58 champion Hawks). Three previous seasons with San Francisco, time that included the presence of Wilt Chamberlain, prepared him for the Philly assignment. With four former Syracuse squad members (Costello, Gambee, Greer and Walker), the main ingredients for Hannum's success were in place. Just add Billy Cunningham, Luke Jackson, Wali Jones, Bob Weiss and a touch of Matt Guokas and Bill Melchionni—oops, almost forgot Chamberlain—and one could anticipate a measure of achievement, and it came in the form of the 1966–67 championship!

The team started the season at 46-4, still the best fifty-game start on record, and finished it at 68-13, the best in league history at the time. Statistically, they were the team to beat, but nobody could—not Cincinnati, Boston or San Francisco, all of whom met them during the playoffs.

As the years passed, Philadelphia would deliver many great moments, some even during visits to Syracuse. On Saturday, January 23, 1965, a special treat came in the form of a 104–100 victory over Boston—putting an end to a sixteen-game wining streak—and happening, of all places, inside the War Memorial. But Philadelphia was still 250 miles from Syracuse—too far for many, too painful for most.

The last member of the Syracuse contingent to score a point in the NBA was Chet Walker, who at age thirty-four finished his career with Chicago during the 1974–75 season. With that last basket, Chet Walker put an end to an era but not to a memory. In Central New York, there will always be 24 seconds left!

PART III
The Syracuse Legacy

Chapter 9

THE 24-SECOND CLOCK

As the 1953–54 season concluded, the future of the five-year-old NBA was questionable. Concerns had arisen regarding the departure of the game's biggest star, George Mikan, and how that would affect the popularity of the game. Ironic, actually, since the game had been modified to negate his effectiveness. Falling from seventeen teams just five years ago to nine might be a natural attrition rate to some, but it can be scary to a professional basketball team owner. Competition, which can increase in a smaller field, is not always guaranteed, nor is the caliber of play. Quality participation at a brisk pace is what appealed to basketball enthusiasts, not teams more concerned about protecting a lead. Entertaining fans, the league's lifeblood, needed to remain paramount.

On Wednesday, November 22, 1950, inside the Minneapolis Auditorium, in a game between the visiting Fort Wayne Zollner Pistons and the Minneapolis Lakers, the expected (and not improbable) happened. The final score between two professional teams playing in the National Basketball Association was 19–18. Now this wasn't just between any two teams—both squads were loaded with formidable talent, from the Lakers' center George Mikan to the capable Piston pivot man Larry Foust. There was no cogency or plausibility associated with the performance; it was simply deplorable.

Pistons coach Murray Mendenhall—frustrated by the Lakers success, as nearly everyone in the league was at that time—decided to implement a stalling strategy to neutralize his opponent's advantage. From the opening tip, this became apparent to everyone from the 2 officials on the court to the

The 24-second "Shot Clock" as it appears inside the Naismith Memorial Basketball Hall of Fame in Springfield, Massachusetts.

7,021 in attendance. When the first quarter ended, Fort Wayne was up 8–7, but by the half their lead had been overturned, advantage Lakers, 13–11.

When the final buzzer sounded, ending the lowest-scoring game in the history of the NBA, reactions varied; however, most fans were actually relieved. "I think it set a record for passing," stated one unidentified observer, while others were not so kind, furious that they had spent money to watch nothing more than a practice. "I got up to get something to drink and when I returned to my seat it was still the same score," spoke another anonymous onlooker. One critic, *Minneapolis Tribune* columnist Dick Cullum—professional basketball is filled with detractors—actually defended it as a masterful display of basketball tactics.

League president Maurice Podoloff believed that the game alienated fans and was conducted in an inappropriate manner. Professional basketball was supposed to be brisk and exhilarating, not prolonged and insipid. Action needed to be taken and considered quickly. But without a time clock, this swiftness could signify, say, four years!

The 24-Second Clock

Enter Danny Biasone, the intuitive owner of the Syracuse Nationals, who knew that this was going to happen—the bubble had to burst! The missing element in the game was time, or accountability. Basketball had to answer to the fans and become responsible to preserve its integrity. But selling that premise to the other team owners wouldn't be so easy.

Biasone invited detractors to Syracuse to witness his idea in action on August 10, 1954. Inside the Blodgett Vocational High School gym, off Oswego Street, on a hot and humid afternoon, a slightly cooler gymnasium became a centerpiece. Biasone's alma mater would become a petri dish filled with innovation on this day—the perfect place, he thought, not nearly as uncomfortable as the old Washington Irving School on the other side of town. Future Hall of Famer Dolph Schayes and a band of other local performers played the first game in which each team had to shoot or else relinquish the ball within 24 seconds.

It would be on this day that Biasone would mimic what would become one of the most common scenes reflected in today's basketball theater: someone standing on the sidelines, typically a coach, shouting, "Shoot the

The 24-second "Shot Clock" honors the rule that changed basketball and resides a few steps from the Jefferson Street State Armory in Armory Square.

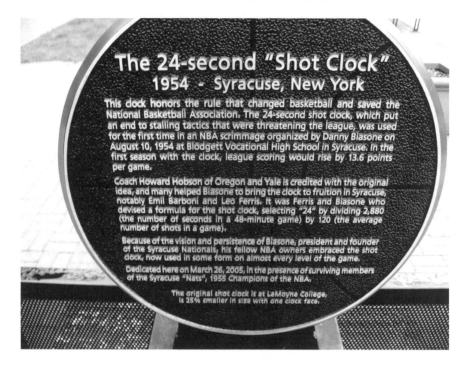

The 24-second "Shot Clock"
1954 - Syracuse, New York

This clock honors the rule that changed basketball and saved the National Basketball Association. The 24-second shot clock, which put an end to stalling tactics that were threatening the league, was used for the first time in an NBA scrimmage organized by Danny Biasone on August 10, 1954 at Blodgett Vocational High School in Syracuse. In the first season with the clock, league scoring would rise by 13.6 points per game.

Coach Howard Hobson of Oregon and Yale is credited with the original idea, and many helped Biasone to bring the clock to fruition in Syracuse, notably Emil Barboni and Leo Ferris. It was Ferris and Biasone who devised a formula for the shot clock, selecting "24" by dividing 2,880 (the number of seconds in a 48-minute game) by 120 (the average number of shots in a game).

Because of the vision and persistence of Biasone, president and founder of the Syracuse Nationals, his fellow NBA owners embraced the shot clock, now used in some form on almost every level of the game.

Dedicated here on March 26, 2005, in the presence of surviving members of the Syracuse "Nats", 1955 Champions of the NBA.

The original shot clock is at LeMoyne College, is 25% smaller in size with one clock face.

A detail of the plaque unveiled on March 26, 2005, in the presence of the surviving members of the Syracuse Nationals.

ball! [counting down the seconds] Shoot the ball!" While NBA elders like Ned Irish of the New York Knicks watched, as did Red Auerbach and Walter A. Brown of the Boston Celtics, most weren't as surprised so much as they were relieved. Many had thought that a clock might be the remedy, but this was actual proof. A few reluctant sighs and a few "I told ya so"s verified the finding.

Player-coach Al Cervi, whistle in tow, oversaw the scrimmage. Various scoreboard companies invited by the league observed—prototypes naturally in hand. There were concerns, however: Cervi with the impact on his players; designers for the repercussions of their inventions; and the owners for the transformation of the game. All were valid and addressed. All-American Scoreboards of Pardeeville, Wisconsin, which had been invited by the league, was given the nod of approval for its accomplishment—a streamlined timepiece befitting a league's rite of passage.

Why 24 seconds? Using the previous three seasons' worth of data, Biasone took the number of shots taken during a typical game into consideration first. He then divided that figure, 120 (shots), into 2,880 seconds, or a forty-eight-minute game. Based on what the current productivity was, he thought, the figure of 24 would not be too restrictive. As it proved, Biasone was correct.

The proof of effectiveness came in productivity, which soared from 79.5 PPG to 93.1 during the 1954–55 season, a difference of 13.6 points. The Boston Celtics even became the first team to average more than 100.0 points per game—an astonishing feat.

The adoption of the shot clock was the most significant change ever made to the game of basketball and was paramount to its survival. It revived the sport and brought the Syracuse Nationals—the first benefactors of its introduction—their first and only championship and Danny Biasone the recognition he so richly deserved.

Chapter 10

THE CALLS FROM SPRINGFIELD

It was our first president, George Washington, who selected Springfield, Massachusetts, as the site of the National Armory—makes you think for a second doesn't it? By the 1780s, it was a major ammunition and weapons depot. The name "Springfield Rifle," a great name for a power forward by the way, was often applied to any sort of arms produced by the Springfield Armory. During that same time period, poor farmers from western Massachusetts, led by Daniel Shays (that's Shays, not Schayes), tried to capture the arms at Springfield. This came to be known as Shays's Rebellion—a term that predates Wilt Chamberlain—and was a key event leading to the Federal Constitutional Convention. All right, "Nuf'ced!" as they say here in Massachusetts; the beautiful city of Springfield is the largest city on the Connecticut River and home to the Naismith Memorial Basketball Hall of Fame, as well it should be.

The hoops institution was established in 1959 by Lee Williams, a former athletic director at Colby College, and it opened its first public facility at Springfield College in Springfield, Massachusetts, in 1968. As anticipated, the response to the site was enthusiastic, and a new building, off-campus, was opened near downtown Springfield in 1985. In 2002, a spectacular $45 million, eighty-thousand-square-foot building designed by New York City architects Gwathmey Siegel & Associates was erected and opened next door, replacing the previous facility. It is a powerful sight, with a basketball reaching toward the sky, as it sits majestically along the riverbank; Dr. Naismith would be proud!

A winter silhouette of the Naismith Memorial Basketball Hall of Fame in Springfield, Massachusetts.

Our exclusive Central New York tour of professional basketball's shrine begins here, so put your admission ticket in your back pocket and take the elevator up to the third floor—the top floor—to step inside a sphere that will send chills up your spine.

I first heard of Vic Hanson from Syracuse University alum James Arthur Ridlon, who raved about his speed and athletic prowess. Ridlon, born on July 11, 1934, in Nanuet, New York, was himself a gifted athlete who spent eight seasons in the National Football League. That someone as talented as Ridlon was impressed with Hanson spoke volumes.

STOP ONE: VICTOR A. "VIC" HANSON

ENSHRINED 1960. BORN IN WATERTOWN, NEW YORK. JULY 30, 1903–APRIL 10, 1982.

The only player in sports history to be inducted into both the College Football and the Naismith Memorial Basketball Hall of Fame, Syracuse University legend Vic Hanson captured nine varsity letters and guided the basketball team to a three-year record of 48-7. He was the cornerstone of the 1925–26 team that went 19-1, their only loss being to Penn State, 37–31. His team was also honored as national champions by the Helms Athletic

MEMBER—BASKETBALL HALL OF FAME

Vic Hanson and All-Syracuse Basket Ball Team at State Armory

Syracuse, New York—Vic Hanson signs Gotch Carr and Charlie Lee, of last year's hill team, to new pro basket ball team here in Syracuse. Keeping a promise to fans, Hanson hopes to secure the finest available attractions in an effort to put over pro basketball here in Syracuse.

Foundation, a Los Angeles–based organization used to select national champion teams and make All-America team selections in a number of college sports, including football and basketball. Chosen as the Helms Player of the Year for his senior season, Hanson recorded 280 points—a Syracuse single-season record that remained until 1946. He played professionally with the Cleveland Rosenblums before returning to Central New York to form his own team, the All-Americans of Syracuse. He is the inspiration for Syracuse University's annual Medal of Excellence, a prestigious honor awarded to a former student-athlete or coach. Career highlights: Helms Athletic Foundation Championship with Syracuse, 1926; Helms Athletic Foundation Player of the Year, 1927; named to Grantland Rice's All-Time, All-America Team, 1952; played with ABL's Cleveland Rosenblums/ Syracuse All-Americans, 1927–30.

Borgmann I had known first for his affiliation with baseball, as a scout, manager and minor league ballplayer. When I learned of his brief stint with the famed New York Celtics, needless to say I was impressed. Any man who could play in the shadow of "Dutch" Dehnert, Nat Holman and Joe Lapchick had my attention. To think that he was also court-side, shouting orders to his Syracuse players inside the Jefferson Street Armory, made me wish that I had been born twenty years earlier.

MEMBER—BASKETBALL HALL OF FAME

Borgmann New Nationals Coach

Syracuse, New York—One of basketball's all-time greats, Ben Borgmann, is taking charge of the Syracuse Nationals. Co-owners Dan Biasone and George Mingin are rounding up talent and state that they will spare no effort to develop a winner here in Central New York. Those fans we spoke to, outside the Jefferson Street Armory, delighted in the thought of the former member of the Original Celtics guiding the new team.

STOP TWO: BERNHARD "BENNIE" BORGMANN

ENSHRINED 1961. BORN IN HALEDON, NEW JERSEY. NOVEMBER 22, 1900–NOVEMBER 11, 1978.

A former standout at the University of Notre Dame, Borgmann went on to star professionally with the Kingston (New York) Colonials. His speed and superior ball handling were his hallmarks, but so was his aggressive attitude. As professional basketball's supreme scorer during the 1920s, Borgmann also played with the Fort Wayne Hoosiers, Chicago Bruins, Brooklyn Americans and Newark Mules. So familiar a hardwood figure was he that opposing players would often joke that if they didn't know an individual on the court, it was likely Borgmann. While playing in the American, Metropolitan and New York State Leagues, he compiled an astounding fifteen scoring titles. He simply loved playing the game—no better exemplified than by picking up two professional titles in the same year, 1923. The transition from prolific basketball player to player-coach to just coach seemed only natural and took place during the 1930s. Of parallel interest to Borgmann was baseball. Most Central New Yorkers recall him for his affiliation with the St. Louis Cardinals organization, although he did manage to play two games for the Syracuse Chiefs in 1941. The Syracuse Nationals of the NBL became his family, and the court inside the Jefferson Street Armory was his fall and winter home in 1946; he also managed baseball clubs alongside his hardwood responsibilities. Career highlights: Premier and prolific guard during the '20s; recipient fifteen scoring titles with various leagues, 1922–35; led both the Paterson Legionnaires and Kingston Colonials to league titles in 1923; played in nearly three thousand basketball games.

I first recall Dolph Schayes, and his wife Naomi, walking through the Fayetteville-Manlius (FM) gymnasium prior to a 1975 varsity basketball game between FM and Jamesville-Dewitt—a team that included their son Danny. A nervous wreck due to their presence, I could barely announce the game—my insignificant duty at the time. After the game—in which FM won 66–59 in a contest that found Danny sidelined with an injured hand—Dolph came over to FM coach Walt Munze's bench and shook the hands of the starters: Brad Over, Jim Devoy, Tom Tramutola, John Mattioli and Jim Bird. "Good game boys!" he spoke. The hardwood legend exemplified every bit the class and dignity I had heard about him. Dolph Schayes—my heart still skips a beat when I hear his name.

MEMBER—BASKETBALL HALL OF FAME

Schayes Nets 47 in Nats Win Over Philly

S
C
H
A
Y
E
S

Syracuse, New York—The Warriors could not stop Dolph Schayes or his team, as the Nationals defeated Philadelphia, 112–86, inside the War Memorial. The Sunday crowd enjoyed watching Schayes drive relentlessly through the lane, attack from the outside or strike efficiently from the charity stripe.

The Nats, who lost to the same Warriors, 98–85, in Camden, New Jersey, on Saturday, delighted in their first victory of March.

STOP THREE: ADOLPH "DOLPH" SCHAYES

ENSHRINED 1973. BORN IN NEW YORK, NEW YORK. MAY 19, 1928.

Around the basket, the six-foot-eight Dolph Schayes was as comfortable on a court as Fred Astaire was on a stage and equally as elegant. Under Hall of Fame coach Howard Cann at New York University (1944–48), Schayes popularized the "city game" while starring in it, exuding every bit of the on-court charisma for which he would later be noted. His dedication was apparent in all elements of his game but perhaps most noteworthy from the foul line, where he often shared league supremacy—he led the NBA in free throw shooting three times—with fellow marksman Bill Sharman. Integral to the transformation of the league into a major sport, Schayes was as permanent and prolific as he was proficient. Upon retirement in 1964, he had played in 1,059 games, more than any other player in NBA history; he was also the NBA's all-time leading scorer with 19,249 points. (Note: In contrast, that figure is higher than that of *any* player who has ever played at both Syracuse University and in the National Basketball Association.) Career highlights: All-America at NYU, 1949; twelve-time NBA All-Star, 1951–62; All-NBA First-Team, 1952–55, 1957–58; NBA Championship with Syracuse Nationals, 1955.

For many of us, those early NBA All-Star Games were something special; without cable or satellite television, we had limited opportunities to see many of the game's greatest stars. On Tuesday, January 23, 1968, the NBA All-Star Game was held in front of 18,422 fans at Madison Square Garden. The familiar face of Alex Hannum was coaching the East, while Bill Sharman was coaching the West. Remembering Chris Schenkel and Jack Twyman calling the game, I was impressed when I learned that the smallest man on the East squad (at six foot two) hit eight field goals without a miss on his way to twenty-one points. While moved by the production, I was later stunned to learn that he only played for seventeen minutes! That man was Philadelphia's Hal Greer. His performance earned him the MVP award and led the East to a 144–124 victory.

STOP FOUR: HAROLD E. "HAL" GREER

ENSHRINED 1982. BORN IN HUNTINGTON, WEST VIRGINIA. JUNE 26, 1936.

Blessed with a "sweet touch" with the basketball, Hal Greer handled it more like a Fabergé egg than a scoring vehicle. He became the first African

MEMBER—BASKETBALL HALL OF FAME

Greer Expected to Break More Nats Records

Syracuse, New York—After only four seasons with the Nationals, Hal Greer holds a number of club records, including most points (39) and field goals (18) for one half and most points (19) for one period at home. The sleek Marshall graduate filled the gap left by an injured Larry Costello last season with a scoring average over 27 points per game, including five straight games of 30 or more points.

American to play for a major college team when he hit the floor for Marshall University. Armed with a deadly one-handed jump shot, Greer help set Marshall's career record for field goal percentage (.545) while impressing many West Virginia fans. He was named All-Conference in 1957 and 1958 and All-America in 1958 before being drafted by the Syracuse Nationals in the second round (sixth pick, thirteenth overall) of the 1958 NBA draft. At the time of his enshrinement, he ranked among the top ten all-time in points scored (21,586), field goals attempted (18,811), field goals made (8,504), minutes played (39,788) and personal fouls (3,825). Suffice it to say that no record was safe while he was playing. In a fifteen-year career, Greer averaged 19.2 PPG—eight seasons of 20.0 PPG or more—while recording 4,540 career assists. His trademark "jump shot free throw" garnered him more than 4,500 points alone. Career highlights: NBA All-Star, 1961–70; NBA Championship with Rochester Royals, 1951; NBA All-Star Game MVP, 1968; NBA 50th Anniversary Team, 1996.

Hailing from the streets of Buffalo, his arms became his most useful weapons; moving, slicing, elbowing, Al Cervi knew all the tricks. He had hands as fast, and as powerful, as some of Buffalo's finest pugilists, but he was taller and I think quicker. Cervi was also an "old-school" cager, worth the price of admission just to hear "Digger" scream, "Hit the bangboards boys! Hit the bangboards!"

STOP FIVE: ALFRED N. "AL" CERVI

ENSHRINED 1985. BORN IN BUFFALO, NEW YORK. FEBRUARY 12, 1917–NOVEMBER 9, 2009.

Nobody was surprised when Al Cervi's aggressive style of play caught the eye of the National Basketball League's newly formed Buffalo Bisons. He was, after all, as acute as he was antagonistic. During the franchise's brief existence, he validated his affection for the game before confirming his love for his country. After five years in the U.S. Army Air Force, "Digger" joined the Rochester Royals, where he captured a league title (1945–46). Quickly establishing himself as a star, Cervi's defensive prowess was exemplary, his offense volatile. As the 1947 NBL Most Valuable Player, Cervi led all scoring with 632 points. Instead of jumping to the BAA the following year with the Royals, a salary dispute took him farther east to Syracuse. There, as player-coach of the Nationals, Cervi thrived while refining his prodigious playing skills. His teams, three of which found their way into the finals, were playoff perennials, always competitive. Retiring as a player in 1953, Cervi continued to coach and motivate his players, even propelling them to a league title in 1955. While it seemed like his heart was always west of Central New York, in Rochester, the city of Syracuse

MEMBER—BASKETBALL HALL OF FAME

NATIONALS WIN SERIES!

Thrilling Victory in Finale, 92–91, Sends Fort Wayne Home!

Syracuse, New York—With a stunning one-point victory during game seven, the Nationals captured the league championship series on Sunday. A confident Coach Cervi guided his Syracuse team against the unrelenting Pistons for four hard-fought quarters inside the War Memorial Auditorium. The capacity crowd was on the edge of their seats as no basket was unanswered by either team until the final seconds ticked off the clock.

adored and respected him dearly. Career highlights: All-NBL First-Team, 1947, 1948, 1949; NBL MVP, 1947; NBL Coach of the Year, 1949; NBA Championship with Syracuse Nationals, 1955.

During the 1969–70 basketball season, Topps, the trading card company, produced a ninety-nine-card set, in ten-card packs. It was the company's first major basketball card set since 1957. For kids growing up during this time period, basketball was just beginning to make an impact, so these oversized cards with the player's photo in an oval frame were considered a novelty. Living in Binghamton at the time, it was a thrill to open one of these packs and find a Dave Bing card—his rookie card—because he had played at Syracuse University. The card was an affirmation that our college hero had made it to the "big time," or as we called it, "Bing Time."

STOP SIX: DAVID "DAVE" BING

ENSHRINED 1990. BORN IN WASHINGTON, D.C. NOVEMBER 24, 1943.

A backcourt wizard, a "king" on his court—that's what they called Dave Bing, a sharp shooter with a marksmen's eye for opportunity and the will to capitalize on it. Hailing from the streets of our nation's capital, he became

MEMBER—BASKETBALL HALL OF FAME

Dave Bing Remembers His College Days

Syracuse, New York—It was his senior year at Syracuse, and Dave Bing fondly recalls his being named the school's first consensus All-American in thirty-nine years. Having averaged an astounding 24.8 points per game in his collegiate career—which included a 28.4 mark as a senior—Bing pushed boundaries never before touched by any player in school history.

Syracuse University's first consensus All-America in 1966 and also the nation's fifth leading scorer (28.4 PPG). Bing was named as one of the top fifty players in NBA history—not for his showmanship, but for his dedication to the fundamentals. As the NBA's Rookie of the Year in 1967, the future mayor of the city of Detroit (sixty-second) had no idea what a legacy he would establish. Twelve NBA seasons with three teams (Detroit Pistons, Washington Bullets and Boston Celtics) saw him average 20.0 points or more seven times. Bing was also named MVP of the '76 All-Star Game. Career highlights: All-America at Syracuse University, 1966; NBA All-Star, 1968–69, 1971–76; All-NBA First-Team, 1968, 1971; NBA 50th Anniversary All-Time Team, 1996.

For most Central New Yorkers, our first encounter with George "Bird" Yardley was as a member of the Fort Wayne Pistons—memorable during the 1955 championship against the Nats, legendary when he became the first player in history to score 2,000 points in one season (with the Detroit Pistons). His prolific point mark, which broke the 1,932-point record held by fellow Hall of Famer George Mikan, seemed predestined for the unstoppable Yardley. As mechanical on the court as he was off (while operating his engineering company), fans getting his autograph outside the War Memorial Auditorium used to marvel at the detailed construction of each letter in his signature.

MEMBER—BASKETBALL HALL OF FAME

Y
A
R
D
L
E
Y

George Yardley to Join the Nationals

Syracuse, New York—The Pistons have traded veteran George Yardley to Syracuse for Ed Conlin. Yardley, who was drafted by Fort Wayne in 1950, scored a league-record 2,001 points, averaging 27.8 points per game in 1957–58. The former mark of 1,932 points, set during the 1950–51 season, was held by Minneapolis center George Mikan. It was Yardley who led the Pistons to the 1954–55 league finals against the Nationals.

STOP SEVEN: GEORGE H. YARDLEY

ENSHRINED 1996. BORN IN HOLLYWOOD, CALIFORNIA. NOVEMBER 3, 1928–
AUGUST 12, 2004.

George "Yardbird" (or "Bird") Yardley was a "point producer," a man
determined to never allow his team to be taken out of a contest. He was
a dangerous clutch performer who was as flamboyant as he was prolific.
During an energetic seven-year professional career (9,063 points, 19.2 PPG),
Yardley appeared in six All-Star Games, averaging just under 20.0 PPG.
At six foot five, the vaulting forward—playing for Fort Wayne, Detroit and
Syracuse—was dangerous every second of a game. With Fort Wayne, Yardley
twice reached the league finals, the most memorable of which were the seven
hard-fought games of the 1955 series against Syracuse. Career highlights:
NBA All-Star, 1955–60; led the NBA in scoring in 1957–58 with an average
of 27.8 points per game; All-NBA First-Team, 1958; AAU Championship
and MVP honors with the San Francisco Stewart Chevrolets, 1951.

*Often identified with coaching the Wilt Chamberlain–led Philadelphia 76ers to the 1966–
67 NBA Championship, Alex Hannum ended the eight-year title streak of the Boston
Celtics. Twelve Hall of Famers played for him, and the most common description that you
hear associated with his name is "well liked." Everyone in Syracuse would certainly agree.*

STOP EIGHT: ALEXANDER M. "ALEX" HANNUM

ENSHRINED 1998. BORN IN LOS ANGELES, CALIFORNIA. JULY 19, 1923–JANUARY
18, 2002.

Transforming floundering teams into champions, Hannum had the Midas
touch, gaining instant respect and credibility with just his presence. Coaching
sixteen professional seasons (twelve NBA and four ABA), he became the first
coach in professional history to win both an NBA and ABA Championship.
Under Hall of Fame coach Sam Barry at the University of Southern California,
his solid performance as a player led him to the National Basketball League
and the NBA (1949–57). As a player-coach, during the 1956–57 season for St.
Louis, Hannum immediately impressed—his team losing in the finals, to the
Celtics, by only two points in game seven. Assuming full-time coaching duties

MEMBER—BASKETBALL HALL OF FAME

New Nats Coach a Familiar Face, Alex Hannum

Syracuse, New York—Former Syracuse player Alex Hannum has been chosen as the Nats' new leader. A graduate of the University of Southern California, Hannum played two seasons for the Nationals before being traded with Fred Scolari to Baltimore for Red Rocha (1951).

Team president Dan Biasone confirmed that he had talked to no one else during the selection process.

the following year, he guided St. Louis to the 1958 NBA Championship. Less than a decade later, he also led the 1966–67 Philadelphia 76ers, considered one of the greatest teams in NBA history, to the same pinnacle. Career highlights: AAU Championship with the Wichita Vickers, 1959; NBA Coach of the Year, 1964; ABA Coach of the Year (coached the ABA's Oakland Oaks from last place to an ABA Championship), 1969; coached both NBA and ABA Championship teams.

Having had many friends who lived in the beautiful Eastwood neighborhood of Syracuse, I consider myself fortunate. When I think of Danny Biasone, I often recall driving by the Eastwood Sports Center with a college friend of mine, Michael Romeo, whose wonderful family happened to live just beyond Shop City. Romeo, as knowledgeable on sports as he was about his community, enlightened me often about Biasone. Not originally from Syracuse, I was ignorant to the rich culture, lifestyle and wonderful charm of the area. A pass through the neighborhood today makes me jealous of those I have met who have had an opportunity to experience that history firsthand.

MEMBER—BASKETBALL HALL OF FAME

Daniel Biasone—Shot Clock Visionary

Syracuse, New York—For Daniel Biasone, the president of the Syracuse Nationals, his legacy may be a clock—a 24-second variety. Biasone, like many other professional basketball team owners, was getting tired of the stall tactics employed by a leading team. Something had to be done, and done quickly, to revive spectator interest in the game. So the Central New York resident took the average total number of shots in a game and divided it into the total number of seconds to create a shot clock timer.

STOP NINE: DANIEL "DANNY" BIASONE

ENSHRINED 2000. BORN IN MIGLIAŃICO, CHIETI, ITALY. FEBRUARY 22, 1909– MAY 25, 1992.

A tough but fair man, Danny Biasone brought professional basketball into Central New York, where it flourished for seventeen extraordinary years. Treating his players as if they were his own sons—some of whom even named a son after him, like Dolph Schayes—Biasone entertained from his players' second home, the Eastwood Sports Center, a neighborhood bowling alley and restaurant. Posting winning records in eleven of fourteen NBA seasons, which included a 1955 NBA Championship, the Syracuse Nationals were perennial playoff participants, one of the last minor market teams. Beloved by a community who witnessed firsthand his sense of responsibility over profit, Biasone resisted numerous tempting purchase offers from large metropolitan markets. A cherished personality, Danny Biasone will forever be remembered in 24-second increments. Career highlights: president and founder, Syracuse Nationals, 1946–63; inventor of the 24-second shot clock, 1954; NBA Championship with Syracuse Nationals, 1955; recipient, John Bunn Award, Naismith Memorial Basketball Hall of Fame, 1982.

While Brooklyn had Jackie Robinson, Syracuse had Earl Lloyd and was equally as proud and grateful for the opportunity. While Lloyd has stated numerous times that he encountered virtually no racist treatment from his teammates and opponents during his decade (1950– 60) in the NBA, he confirmed that fans were not so tolerant. Sometimes in life you need courage, and Earl Lloyd exhibited plenty.

STOP TEN: EARL F. LLOYD

ENSHRINED 2003. BORN IN ALEXANDRIA, VIRGINIA. APRIL 3, 1928.

As one of three African Americans to enter the NBA at the same time, it was only because of the order in which the teams' season openers fell that Earl Lloyd was the first of his ethnic origin to play in a league game. On the night of October 31, 1950—one day ahead of Cooper of the Boston Celtics and four days before Clifton of the New York Knicks—Earl Lloyd, a forward with the Washington Capitols, made history. In an era of segregation, he conducted himself with exemplary style, both on and off the court. "The Big Cat" distinguished himself as a two-time All-America selection at West Virginia State while leading his team to an undefeated 30-0 season (1947–48),

MEMBER—BASKETBALL HALL OF FAME

Lloyd Superb in Championship Season

Syracuse, New York—On a cold day in January 1951, the Nationals selected Earl Lloyd from Washington in the dispersal draft. Having only appeared in seven professional games for the Capitols, little was known about the West Virginia State University standout. Averaging 10.2 points and 7.7 rebounds during the Nationals' 1954–55 championship season, Syracuse fans soon realized what a treasure they had acquired.

a conference championship and an unofficial "national champions" status. During nine seasons, with the Capitols, Nationals and Pistons, he mastered his defensive skills—best exemplified during the 1955 Syracuse championship campaign. Career highlights: named CIAA "Player of the Decade" for the 1940s; National Association of Intercollegiate Athletes (NAIA) Silver and Golden Anniversary Teams; member of NBA Championship team, 1955; first African American bench coach, 1968.

A tenable coach, certainly to Syracuse basketball fans, Jim Boeheim ("The Master of the Zone Defense") has been the subject of nearly a half-century transformation, from walk-on basketball player and able instructor to quality coach and basketball legend. To Syracuse basketball enthusiasts, who empathize with this man, he is not only their mentor but is also the greatest college basketball coach of all time. The community not only loves him for his believability, hardwood success and altruism but also for his accessibility—he has never shunned them and has always been congenial and a role model.

STOP ELEVEN: JIM BOEHEIM

ENSHRINED 2005. BORN IN LYONS, NEW YORK. NOVEMBER 17, 1944.

Jim Boeheim and Syracuse University have become synonymous, and rightfully so, as no single man has brought more enjoyment to college basketball's premier fans than this humble man from Lyons, New York. Enrolling at Syracuse in the fall of 1962 was perhaps his destiny, and it came in a shade of orange. But fate, being distance-limited, left the walk-on freshman a challenge in perseverance. Serving as a respected co-captain with fellow Hall of Famer Dave Bing, he answered that provocation; the duo's efforts yielded the program's second NCAA tournament berth. After serving as an assistant, Boeheim was appointed head coach in 1976. At the time of his Springfield enshrinement, he had guided Syracuse to its first NCAA Championship (2003), three Final Four appearances (1987, 1996 and 2003) and more than seven hundred wins. The winningest coach in Big East history, Boeheim has also been active with USA Basketball and has served as part of many different coaching staffs that have garnered gold during international competition. As a humanitarian, his leadership role with Coaches vs. Cancer is exemplary of the guiding principles that govern his life. He has been a gift to Central New York, one we treasure, and a

MEMBER—BASKETBALL HALL OF FAME

NATIONAL CHAMPIONS!

Syracuse Defeats Kansas, 81–78!

Syracuse, New York—Coach Jim Boeheim has won his national championship! The title, which eluded him in both 1987 and 1996, evades him no longer. A dedicated Syracuse team, led by Carmelo Anthony—the 2003 tournament's Most Outstanding Player—played their hearts out. Knocking a Michael Lee three-point attempt out of bounds during the final seconds, sophomore Hakim Warrick helped Syracuse hold on to its first NCAA Championship.

BOEHEIM

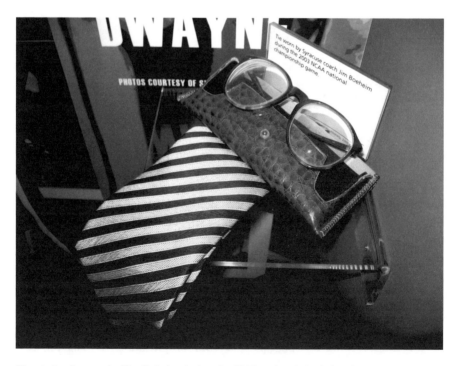

Here is the tie worn by Jim Boeheim during the 2003 national championship game, as well as a pair of his glasses with case. This display appears inside the Naismith Memorial Basketball Hall of Fame.

person we will never forget. Career highlights: national championship at Syracuse, 2003; Big East Conference Coach of the Year, 1984, 1991, 2000, 2010; three NCAA Final Fours, 1987, 1996, 2003; USA Basketball National Coach of the Year; 2001, the Associated Press College Basketball Coach of the Year, 2010; Naismith 2010 College Coach of the Year.

STOP TWELVE: YOUR SELECTION!

There are so many wonderful memories preserved in Springfield that to dictate a final stop on your tour would be inappropriate, so choose an individual we failed to mention. Look all around you. Basketball doesn't just build character, it reveals it!

Chapter 11
PROFESSIONAL BASKETBALL, SYRACUSE STYLE

If loyalty defines a basketball enthusiast, then intense devotion explains a Syracuse sports fan. His adherence, or sentiment of attachment, can be to an individual, such as Dolph Schayes, or to a group, such as the Nationals, but it can also be a form of duty, be it geographic ties or academics. It can even be to a cause, like the sport itself, basketball, and its preferred result, winning. Expressed through thought and action, a fan yearns for identification with his subject.

Fanaticism, a rare sequel to loyalty, can become uncontrolled—Nats fans remember "The Strangler"—but that is not preferred. Instead, decorum in the form of resignation, or reluctant acceptance, may be a more suitable option; ok, forgive, but never forget!

For some basketball fans, homage can stir or arouse or even bring meaning, direction and purpose into their lives, all while integrating their activities. For zealots of the game, devotion has a social function. If it did not, things like "tailgating" or "Fan Clubs" would not exist. Charlatans do not come in orange—no disambiguation needed.

As the Nationals packed up their belongings inside the War Memorial and departed Central New York, basketball fans looked for alternatives. "We obviously knew about college basketball on the hill," recalls Ford Baker. "Billy Gabor was one of our favorite players and all he had to do after graduation was walk down the hill." Such was indeed the case, as not only were fans aware of Gabor, but some knew others as well. Jack Kiley had played with Fort Wayne, Edwin Miller had gone to Baltimore via

Milwaukee, Franklin Reddout had played with Rochester and Lou Spicer had even played a bit at Providence (BAA)—hoops intelligentsia rule in Orange Country! Professional basketball had ties right here at home with, or in this case without, the Nationals. Accepting the fact that those links would now correlate to the early years of a player's development, and not to a mature professional, might be an objection—a factor that *could* determine a fan's level of satisfaction.

Allegiance to any sports team is difficult to maintain from both sides of the equation. It is affected by factors such as the passage of time, a team's success or failure, changes in team personnel, the movement of a franchise and, of course, an individual's general interest in the sport. But if fans love a game such as basketball, they will find recourse, be it a cost-effective solution or an expensive alternative. While an identical substitute would be perfect, even hoops fans in major markets, such as metropolitan New York, know that the Knickerbockers are not the Nets, and vice versa. Options have tradeoffs, commonly in price versus performance—a factor most of us know and understand.

Since a passionate love for a game can't be denied, certainly not in Central New York, Syracuse basketball fans turned to a place where they had found solace before: college basketball.

Changing Faces, Changing Times

In their final season, the Nationals had the War Memorial all to themselves; they had been sharing their court with Syracuse basketball coach Marc Gully's squad while a new facility was being constructed. It was a bit of professional propinquity given the circumstances. Fred Lewis (1962–68) then took over the coaching duties and helped christen the George L. Manley Field House during the 1962–63 season. Guiding his team into the NIT in 1964, Lewis then took the Dave Bing–led 1965–66 squad to the NCAA tournament. Oh yes, that lanky kid in the front row of that team picture—no, not Rex Trowbridge—number 35; that's a young Jim Boeheim. For Syracuse basketball fans, there were plenty of reasons to look to a resplendent hill, replete with talent.

During a six-year span (1964–70), fans could also enjoy an occasional visit from Philadelphia. They were not just any events; they were genuine contests. Games like Wilt Chamberlain's "deadeye" victory over Oscar Robertson and Cincinnati on February 28, 1967, were welcomed inside the War Memorial. It was an event that saw the giant score twenty-eight points and extract thirty-six rebounds. Chamberlain even made his first four shots from the floor, setting a league record of thirty-five consecutive field goals without a miss. However, while it may have been numinous splendor from a king on his court, the front of his uniform did not read "Nats."

Manley Field House quickly became a safe haven for players and a new wave of fans. They were descendants of Coliseum warriors and War Memorial survivors. "Manley was our Astrodome," spoke an elder statesman. "It seemed like we never lost in the building" (the actual record: 190-30).

Coach Roy Danforth (1968–76) took the reins from Fred Lewis and never looked back, ushering his team to its first NCAA Final Four appearance in 1974–75. Danforth also drove two of his clubs to the NIT and then his last four squads to the NCAA tournament—a portentous precursor indeed! When he departed for Tulane in 1976, an assistant stepped up, and his name was Jim Boeheim (1976–present).

When a new conference was formed, on May 31, 1979, it quickly emerged as one of the premier "big" leagues in college basketball's East, the perfect prelude to the excitement generated by the opening of the Dome (Carrier) the following year. Hardwood gladiators now had their coliseum and hoops fans their utopia—had Sir Thomas More played basketball, it would have been in a shade of reddish-yellow. Forever sharing the common denominator of loyalty, generations of fans—most of whom still break out in a rash at the very mention of Red Auerbach, Bob Cousy, either John Thompson (John R. Thompson Jr. and John Thompson III) or Keith Smart—continue to share basketball history in Syracuse, their "Hoops Roots."

INSTITUTIONS AND THEIR PROFESSIONAL INFLUENCE

Player
Span
Teams (in order of appearance)
Statistics

College is Syracuse unless noted. List not intended to be comprehensive.

Rafael Addison
1986/87–1996/97
Phoenix, New Jersey, Detroit, Charlotte
G, 379; PTS, 2,186; AVG, 5.4

Carmelo Anthony
2003–present
Denver

Dave Bing (HOF)
1966/67–1977/78
Detroit, Washington, Boston
G, 901; PTS, 18,327; AVG, 20.3

Jim Boeheim (HOF)
1966/67–1971/72
Scranton—Eastern League

Roosevelt Bouie
Dallas
1980 NBA Draft; chose to play in Italy.

Damone Brown
2001/02–2004/05
Philadelphia, Toronto, New Jersey, Washington
G, 39; PTS, 108; AVG, 3.0

Marty Byrnes
1978/79–1982/83
Phoenix/New Orleans, Los Angeles, Dallas, Indiana
G, 263; PTS, 1,495; AVG, 5.2

Vincent Cohen
Syracuse
1957 NBA Draft; chose not to play.

Derrick Coleman
1990/91–2004/05
New Jersey, Philadelphia, Charlotte, Philadelphia, Detroit
G, 781; PTS, 12,884; AVG, 14.6

Sherman Douglas
1989/90–2000/01
Miami, Boston, Milwaukee, New Jersey, Los Angeles (Clippers), New Jersey
G, 765; PTS, 8,425; AVG, 10.4

Dennis Duval
1974/75–1975/76
Washington, Atlanta
G, 50; PTS, 96; AVG, 2.2

LeRon Ellis
1991/92–1995/96
Los Angeles (Clippers), Charlotte, Miami
G, 81; PTS, 277; AVG, 2.3

Jonny Flynn
2009/10–present
Minnesota

Billy Gabor
1948/49–1954/55
Syracuse
G, 365; PTS, 3,352; AVG, 8.7

Donte Green
2008/09–present
Sacramento

Rudy Hackett
1975/76–1976/77
St. Louis (ABA), New York (Nets)/Indiana
G, 28; PTS, 155; AVG, 4.5

Vic Hanson
1927–30
Cleveland (ABL)

Jason Hart
2000/01–present
Milwaukee, San Antonio, Charlotte, Sacramento, Los Angeles (Clippers), Utah, Los Angeles (Clippers)/Denver
Dave Johnson
1992/93–1993/94
Portland, Chicago
G, 59; PTS, 204; AVG, 3.3

Wes Johnson
2010/11–present
Minnesota

Jack Kiley
1951/52–1952/53
Fort Wayne
G, 53; PTS, 124; AVG, 1.8

Greg Kohls
Buffalo
1972 Draft pick; Washington Generals

Jim Lee
Cleveland
1975 Draft pick; did not play.

Edwin Miller
1952/53–1953/54
Milwaukee, Baltimore
G, 142; PTS, 1,452; AVG, 10.3

Lawrence Moten
1995/96–1996/97
Vancouver
G, 111; PTS, 738; AVG, 6.7

Demetris Nichols
2007/08–2008/09
Cleveland/Chicago, Chicago/New York
G, 18; PTS, 22; AVG, 1.5

Louis Orr
1980/81–1987/88
Indiana, New York
G, 558; PTS, 5,545; AVG, 9.0

Billy Owens
1991/92–2000/01
Golden State, Miami, Sacramento, Seattle, Philadelphia/Golden State, Detroit
G, 600; PTS, 7,026; AVG, 11.3

Andy Rautins
2010/11–present
New York

Leo Rautins
1983/84–1984/85
Philadelphia, Atlanta
G, 32; PTS, 48; AVG, 1.7

Franklin Reddout
1953/54
Rochester
G, 7; PTS, 13; AVG, 1.9

Fred Saunders
1974/75–1977/78
Phoenix, Boston/New Orleans
G, 210; PTS, 1,107; AVG, 4.9

Don Savage (LeMoyne)
1951/52–1956/57
Syracuse
G, 17; PTS, 54; AVG, 3.2

Danny Schayes
1981/82–1998/99
Utah, Denver, Milwaukee, Los Angeles (Lakers), Phoenix, Miami, Orlando
G, 1,138; PTS, 8,780; AVG, 7.7

Joe Schwarzer
Played for a professional team briefly in Syracuse.

Rony Seikaly
1988/89–1998/99
Miami, Golden State, Orlando, New Jersey
G, 678; PTS, 9,991; AVG, 13.0

Wilmeth Sidat-Singh
Played briefly for the Reds, a professional barnstorming basketball team in Syracuse; also the New York Renaissance and Washington Bruins/Lichtman Bears.

Bill Smith
1971/72–1972/73
Portland
G, 30; PTS, 205; AVG, 5.6

Lou Spicer
1946/47
Providence
G, 4; PTS, 1; AVG, 0.3

Etan Thomas
2000/01–present
Dallas, Washington, Oklahoma City

Stephen Thompson
1991/92
Orlando, Sacramento
G, 19; PTS, 31; AVG, 1.6

John Wallace
1996/97–2003/04
New York, Toronto, New York, Detroit, Phoenix, Miami
G, 381; PTS, 2,175; AVG, 9.4

Hakim Warrick
2005/06–present
Memphis, Milwaukee, Chicago

Dwayne Washington
1986/87–1988/89
New Jersey, Miami
G, 194; PTS, 1,660; AVG, 8.5

Darryl Watkins
2007/08
Sacramento
G, 9; PTS, 12; AVG, 1.3

BIBLIOGRAPHY

ARTICLES, ASSOCIATIONS AND RELATED MATERIALS

Central New York Basketball, Inc. Team, player, personnel and financial information. Note: Not all players are listed—only the names the club recognized in its available records.

The Naismith Memorial Basketball Hall of Fame. Records and photography.

National Basketball Association. Programs, media guides and assorted records.

The Syracuse Professional Basketball Club, Inc. Team, player, personnel and financial information. Note: Not all players are listed—only the names the club recognized in its available records.

BOOKS

Araton, Harvey, and Filip Bondy. *The Selling of the Green: The Financial Rise and Moral Decline of the Boston Celtics.* New York: HarperCollins, 1992.

Basloe, Frank J., with D. Gordon Rohman. *I Grew Up with Basketball.* New York: Greenberg, 1952.

Brown, Jim, with Steve Delsohn. *Out of Bounds*. New York: Kensington Publishing Corporation, 1989.

Chamberlain, Wilt, and David Shaw. *WILT*. New York: Macmillan Publishing Company, Inc., 1973.

Gould, Todd. *Pioneers of the Hardwood: Indiana and the Birth of Professional Basketball*. Bloomington: Indiana University Press, 1998.

Hollander, Zander. *The Pro Basketball Encyclopedia*. New York: American Library, 1981.

Holman, Nat. *Holman on Basketball*. New York: Crown Publishers, Inc., 1950.

Koppett, Leonard. *24 Seconds to Shoot*. New York: Macmillan Publishing Company, Inc., 1968.

Lapchick, Joe. *50 Years of Basketball*. Engelwood Cliffs, NJ: Prentice-Hall, 1968.

Mikan, George, and Joseph Oberle. *Unstoppable: The Story of George Mikan, the 1st NBA Superstar*. Indianapolis, IN: Masters Press, 1997.

Nelson, Rodger. *The Zollner Piston Story*. Fort Wayne, IN: Allen County Public Library Foundation, 1995.

Peterson, Robert W. *Cages to Jumpshots: Pro Basketball's Early Years*. New York: Oxford University Press, 1990.

INTERNET SOURCES

Association for Professional Basketball Research. www.apbr.org.

ESPN. http://espn.go.com.

Library of Congress, Prints & Photographs Division. www.loc.gov.

NBA & ABA Basketball Statistics & History. www.basketball-reference.com.

BIBLIOGRAPHY

The *New York Times*. www.nytimes.com.

Salt City Cagers. www.saltcitycagers.com.

Sports Illustrated. http://sportsillustrated.cnn.com.

The *Syracuse Post-Standard*. www.syracuse.com.

Washington City Paper. www.washingtoncitypaper.com.

Wikipedia, the Free Encyclopedia. www.en.wikipedia.org.

JOURNALS

All-Sports News (March 2, 1949).

MAGAZINES

Basketball Digest (March 2003).
LIFE magazine.
SPORT magazine.
SPORTS ILLUSTRATED (December 3, 1962; November 25, 1968).

NEWSPAPERS AND ARTICLES

Albany Democrat-Herald.

Albany Times Union.

Anderson, Dave. "SPORTS OF THE TIMES: Old P.S.A.L. Names Reminisce a Little." *New York Times*, March 10, 2000.

Araton, Harvey. "ON PRO BASKETBALL: Biasone as Visionary Is N.B.A. Loss." *New York Times*, May 28, 1992.

Boston Globe.

Buffalo News.

Goldaper, Sam. "Nat Broudy, 76, Ex-Timekeeper." *New York Times.* Obituary, January 24, 1991.

Goldstein, Richard. "George Yardley, 75, Shooter who broke N.B.A. Record." *New York Times.* Obituary, August 16, 2004.

———. "Haskell Cohen, 86, Publicist; Created N.B.A. All-Star Game." *New York Times.* Obituary, July 3, 2000.

Kirst, Sean. "Eastwood Took Its Shot at NBA Glory." *Syracuse Post-Standard*, November 22, 1999.

McKenna, Dave. "The Syracuse Walking Dream." *Washington City Paper*, May 23, 2008.

New York Daily News.

New York Times. "Charley Eckman; Basketball Coach and Referee, 73." Obituary, July 4, 1995.

———. "Ex-Players Attend Biasone Funeral." May 29, 1992.

———. "Irving Kosloff, 82, Ex-Owner of 76ers." Obituary, February 22, 1995.

———. "Larry Costello, 70, Player and Coach in N.B.A. Dead." Obituary, December 14, 2001.

———. "Leo Ferris, a Founder of N.B.A., Dies at 76." Obituary, June 5, 1993.

———. "Maurice Podoloff, 95." Obituary, November 26, 1985.

———. "Pop Gates, 82." Obituary, December 5, 1995.

———. "SPORTS PEOPLE: Davis Hot Streak." February 27, 1983.

Oregonian. "Red Rocha, 86." Obituary, December 15, 2010.

Paikert, Charles. "Ideas & Trends: The Clock Was Ticking…The Man Who Saved the N.B.A." *New York Times*, May 14, 2000.

Poliquin, Bud. "Finally, All These Years Later, Billy Gabor Will Get His SU Jersey Retired." *Syracuse Post-Standard*, February 28, 2009.

Popper, Steve. "Paul Seymour, 70, Part of N.B.A. Title Team." *New York Times*. Obituary, May 8, 1998.

Press & Sun-Bulletin, Binghamton, New York.

Rhoden, William C. "SPORTS OF THE TIMES: 'Too Late; Fall Back, Baby.'" *New York Times*, February 26, 1991.

Rochester Democrat and Chronicle. "Al Cervi, 92." Obituary, November 10, 2009.

Rochester Herald.

SU Daily Orange (Syracuse University).

Syracuse Herald-Journal, December 1939.

Syracuse Post-Standard, March 27, 1949; March 31, 1954.

Utica Observer Dispatch.

Waitzkin, Fred. "Just a Basketball Guy." *New York Times*, February 11, 1990.

Wright, Gloria. "Signs Saved at Sports Site." *Syracuse Post-Standard*, November 18, 1999.

RADIO, TELEVISION AND ASSORTED VIDEO

Transcripts read and recordings, films and videos reviewed by author.

ESPN—numerous player interviews and archive footage, such as 1954–55 NBA Championship

Rare Sportsfilms, Inc.—1961 and 1962 NBA All-Star Game highlights
WAGE (ABC)
WFBL (CBS)
WHEN
WKJG (Fort Wayne)—1954–55 radio transcripts
WNDR (MBS)
WOLF (Independent)
WSYR (NBC)

REFERENCE SOURCES

Moore, Peter, ed. The 2010 Syracuse University Men's Basketball Guide. Athletic Communications Department, Syracuse University.

ADDITIONAL NOTES AND DISCLAIMERS

Early records can be incomplete or incorrect. Rosters could vary (substitutions were used), some individuals even played for multiple teams and uniform numbers also varied.

Material is not intended to be comprehensive.

All NBA team insignias depicted in this publication (Getty Images) are the property of NBA Properties, Inc. and the respective teams of the NBA.

The Pepsi logo is a registered trademark of PepsiCo Inc.

INDEX

ABOUT THE AUTHOR

Mark Allen Baker is a former business executive (General Electric/ Genigraphics Corporation, assistant to the president and CEO), author (sixteen books and more than two hundred articles) and historian. A graduate of the State University of New York, his expertise has been referenced in numerous periodicals, including *USA Today*, *Sports Illustrated* and *Money*. Following his book, *Goldmine's Price Guide to Rock & Roll Memorabilia*, he appeared as a co-host on the VH1 series *Rock Collectors*. Baker has also been a featured speaker at many events, including the Hemingway Days Festival & Writers Conference in Key West, Florida. He is also the author of the recently (2010) published book *Title Town USA: Boxing in Upstate New York*.

The author can be contacted at PO Box 782, Hebron, CT, 06248.

Visit us at
www.historypress.net